CELTIC

Prayers and Incantations

CELTIC
Prayers and Incantations

Alexander Carmichael

DOVER PUBLICATIONS, INC.
Mineola, New York

Bibliographical Note

This Dover edition, first published in 2007, contains 194 prayers and incantations reprinted from the first two volumes of the six-volume *Carmina Gadelica,* as originally printed for the author by T. and A. Constable, Edinburgh, in 1900. A Publisher's Note has been specially prepared for the present edition.

Library of Congress Cataloging-in-Publication Data

Carmichael, Alexander, 1832–1912.
[Carmina gadelica. English. Selections]
Celtic prayers and incantations / Alexander Carmichael. — Dover ed.
p. cm.
Originally published: Carmina gadelica. Edinburgh : T. and A. Constable, 1900.
ISBN 0-486-45741-9
1. Christian poetry, Scottish Gaelic—Translations into English. 2. Incantations, Scottish Gaelic—Translations into English. 3. Hymns, Scottish Gaelic—Translations into English. 4. Prayers. 5. Incantations. I. Title.

PB1645.C3213 2007
891.6'310080382—dc22

2006102448

Manufactured in the United States of America
Dover Publications, Inc., 31 East 2nd Street, Mineola, N.Y. 11501

Publisher's Note

A lexicon of Gaelic oral literature, the six-volume *Carmina Gadelica* stands as a pious anthology of ancient charms, prayers, and incantations. Its collector and editor, Alexander Carmichael (1832–1912), compiled Gaelic verse and prose from the recitations of individuals from the Highlands and Islands of Scotland during the latter half of the nineteenth century. Witnessing firsthand the moribundity of the Gaelic oral tradition, Carmichael set out to chronicle the rich tapestry of their folk traditions. His conscientious efforts, which cataloged prayers, charms, and songs, have become an enduring reference on Celtic spirituality.

The present edition reprints over 190 prayers and incantations from the first two volumes of *Carmina Gadelica,* the only ones published during Carmichael's own lifetime. From invocations to Jesus, Mary, and the saints to blessings and chants for seasonal observances, the verses selected here are a timeless archive of Scottish and Gaelic folklore. Many of these chants were used in the ritualization of common everyday rural tasks as well as for celebratory rites of passage. Christmas poems and charms for various ailments are also included in this unique heritage of folk poetry handed down orally through countless generations. Through the success of Carmichael's *Carmina Gadelica,* the hopes, dreams, and fears of this now-lost culture have been kept intact for posterity.

Contents

CELTIC
Prayers and Incantations

Invocations

1 Rune before prayer

I am bending my knee
In the eye of the Father who created me,
In the eye of the Son who purchased me,
In the eye of the Spirit who cleansed me,
    In friendship and affection.
Through Thine own Anointed One, O God,
Bestow upon us fullness in our need,
      Love towards God,
      The affection of God,
      The smile of God,
      The wisdom of God,
      The grace of God,
      The fear of God,
      And the will of God
To do on the world of the Three,
As angels and saints
Do in heaven;
      Each shade and light,
      Each day and night,
      Each time in kindness,
      Give Thou us Thy Spirit.

2   God with me lying down

God with me lying down,
God with me rising up,
God with me in each ray of light,
Nor I a ray of joy without Him,
    Nor one ray without Him.

Christ with me sleeping,
Christ with me waking,
Christ with me watching,
Every day and night,
    Each day and night.

God with me protecting,
The Lord with me directing,
The Spirit with me strengthening,
For ever and for evermore,
    Ever and evermore, Amen.
    Chief of chiefs, Amen.

3   The invocation of the graces

I bathe thy palms
In showers of wine,
In the lustral fire,
In the seven elements,
In the juice of the rasps,
In the milk of honey,
And I place the nine pure choice graces
In thy fair fond face,
    The grace of form,
    The grace of voice,
    The grace of fortune,
    The grace of goodness,
    The grace of wisdom,
    The grace of charity,

The grace of choice maidenliness,
The grace of whole-souled loveliness,
The grace of goodly speech.

Dark is yonder town,
Dark are those therein,
Thou art the brown swan,
Going in among them.
Their hearts are under thy control,
Their tongues are beneath thy sole,
Nor will they ever utter a word
      To give thee offence.

A shade art thou in the heat,
A shelter art thou in the cold,
Eyes art thou to the blind,
A staff art thou to the pilgrim,
An island art thou at sea,
A fortress art thou on land,
A well art thou in the desert,
      Health art thou to the ailing.

Thine is the skill of the Fairy Woman,
Thine is the virtue of Bride the calm,
Thine is the faith of Mary the mild,
Thine is the tact of the woman of Greece,
Thine is the beauty of Emir the lovely,
Thine is the tenderness of Darthula delightful,
Thine is the courage of Maebh the strong,
      Thine is the charm of Binne-bheul.

Thou art the joy of all joyous things,
Thou art the light of the beam of the sun,
Thou art the door of the chief of hospitality,
Thou art the surpassing star of guidance,
Thou art the step of the deer of the hill,
Thou art the step of the steed of the plain,
Thou art the grace of the swan of swimming,
      Thou art the loveliness of all lovely desires.

The lovely likeness of the Lord
Is in thy pure face,
The loveliest likeness that
Was upon earth.

The best hour of the day be thine,
The best day of the week be thine,
The best week of the year be thine,
The best year in the Son of God's domain be thine.

Peter has come and Paul has come,
James has come and John has come,
Muriel and Mary Virgin have come,
Uriel the all-beneficent has come,
Ariel the beauteousness of the young has come,
Gabriel the seer of the Virgin has come,
Raphael the prince of the valiant has come,
And Michael the chief of the hosts has come,
    And Jesus Christ the mild has come,
    And the Spirit of true guidance has come,
    And the King of kings has come on the helm,
    To bestow on thee their affection and their love,
        To bestow on thee their affection and their love.

4   A general supplication

God, listen to my prayer,
Bend to me Thine ear,
Let my supplications and my prayers
Ascend to Thee upwards.
Come, Thou King of Glory,
To protect me down,
Thou King of life and mercy
With the aid of the Lamb,
Thou Son of Mary Virgin
To protect me with power,

Thou Son of the lovely Mary
Of purest fairest beauty.

5   God be with us

God be with us
On this Thy day,
       Amen.
God be with us
On this Thy night,
       Amen.
To us and with us,
On this Thy day,
       Amen.
To us and with us,
On this Thy night,
       Amen.
It is clear to be seen of us,
Since we came into the world,
That we have deserved Thy wrath,
       Amen.
O Thine own wrath,
Thou God of all,
       Amen.
Grant us forgiveness,
       Amen.
Grant us forgiveness,
       Amen.
Grant to us Thine own forgiveness,
Thou merciful God of all,
       Amen.
Anything that is evil to us,
Or that may witness against us
Where we shall longest be,
Illume it to us,
Obscure it to us,

Banish it from us,
Root it out of our hearts,
Ever, evermore, everlastingly.
    Ever, evermore, everlastingly.
        Amen.

6   Jesu, Thou Son of Mary

Jesu, Thou Son of Mary,
Have mercy upon us,
        Amen.
Jesu, Thou Son of Mary,
Make peace with us,
        Amen.
Oh, with us and for us
Where we shall longest be,
        Amen.
Be about the morning of our course,
Be about the closing of our life,
        Amen.
Be at the dawning of our life,
And oh! at the dark'ning of our day,
        Amen.
Be for us and with us,
Merciful God of all,
        Amen.
Consecrate us
Condition and lot,
Thou King of kings,
Thou God of all,
        Amen.
Consecrate us
Rights and means,
Thou King of kings,
Thou God of all,
        Amen.

Consecrate us
Heart and body,
Thou King of kings,
Thou God of all,
      Amen.
Each heart and body,
Each day to Thyself,
Each night accordingly,
Thou King of kings,
Thou God of all,
      Amen.

7 Holy Father of glory

Thanks be to Thee, Holy Father of glory,
Father kind, ever-loving, ever-powerful,
Because of all the abundance, favour, and deliverance
That Thou bestowest upon us in our need.
Whatever providence befalls us as thy children,
In our portion, in our lot, in our path,
Give to us with it the rich gifts of Thine hand
And the joyous blessing of Thy mouth.

We are guilty and polluted, O God,
In spirit, in heart, and in flesh,
In thought, in word, in act,
We are hard in Thy sight in sin.
Put Thou forth to us the power of Thy love,
Be thou leaping over the mountains of our transgressions,
And wash us in the true blood of conciliation,
Like the down of the mountains, like the lily of the lake.

In the steep common path of our calling,
Be it easy or uneasy to our flesh,
Be it bright or dark for us to follow,
Thine own perfect guidance be upon us.
Be Thou a shield to us from the wiles of the deceiver,

From the arch-destroyer with his arrows pursuing us,
And in each secret thought our minds get to weave,
Be Thou Thyself on our helm and at our sheet.

Though dogs and thieves would reive us from the fold,
Be Thou the valiant Shepherd of glory near us.
Whatever matter or cause or propensity
That would bring to us grief, or pains, or wounds,
Or that would bear witness against us at the last,
On the other side of the great river of dark shadows,
Oh! do Thou obscure it from our eyes,
And from our hearts drive it for ever.

Now to the Father who created each creature,
Now to the Son who paid ransom for His people,
Now to the Holy Spirit, Comforter of might:
Shield and sain us from every wound;
Be about the beginning and end of our race,
Be giving us to sing in glory,
In peace, in rest, in reconciliation,
Where no tear shall be shed, where death comes no more.
      Where no tear shall be shed, where death comes no more.

8   A prayer

O God,
In my deeds,
In my words,
In my wishes,
In my reason,
And in the fulfilling of my desires,
In my sleep,
In my dreams,
In my repose,
In my thoughts,
In my heart and soul always,

May the blessed Virgin Mary,
And the promised Branch of Glory dwell.
    Oh! in my heart and soul always,
    May the blessed Virgin Mary,
    And the fragrant Branch of Glory dwell.

9   Rune of the *muthairn**

Thou King of the moon,
Thou King of the sun,
Thou King of the planets,
Thou King of the stars,
Thou King of the globe,
Thou King of the sky,
Oh! lovely Thy countenance,
Thou beauteous Beam.

Two loops of silk
Down by thy limbs,
Smooth-skinned;
Yellow jewels
And a handful
Out of every stock of them.

10   Bless, O Chief of generous chiefs

Bless, O Chief of generous chiefs,
Myself and everything anear me,
Bless me in all my actions,
Make Thou me safe for ever,
    Make Thou me safe for ever.

---

*Little mother, dear little mother.

From every brownie and ban-shee,
From every evil wish and sorrow,
From every nymph and water-wraith,
From every fairy-mouse and grass-mouse,
    From every fairy-mouse and grass-mouse.

From every troll among the hills,
From every siren hard pressing me,
From every ghoul within the glens,
Oh! save me till the end of my day.
    Oh! save me till the end of my day.

11   The guiding light of eternity

O God, who broughtst me from the rest of last night
Unto the joyous light of this day,
Be Thou bringing me from the new light of this day
Unto the guiding light of eternity.
    Oh! from the new light of this day
    Unto the guiding light of eternity.

12   A prayer for grace

I am bending my knee
In the eye of the Father who created me,
In the eye of the Son who died for me,
In the eye of the Spirit who cleansed me,
    In love and desire.

Pour down upon us from heaven
The rich blessing of Thy forgiveness;
Thou who art uppermost in the City,
    Be Thou patient with us.

Grant to us, Thou Saviour of Glory,
The fear of God, the love of God, and His affection,
And the will of God to do on earth at all times
As angels and saints do in heaven;
Each day and night give us Thy peace.
    Each day and night give us Thy peace.

13   Prayer for protection

As Thou art the Shepherd over the flock
Tend Thou us to the cot and the fold,
Sain us beneath Thine own glorious mantle;
    Thou Shield of protection, guard us for ever.

Be Thou a hard triumphant glave
To shield us securely from wicked hell,
From the fiends and from the stieve snell gullies,
    And from the lurid smoke of the abyss.

Be my soul in the trustance of the High King,
Be Michael the powerful meeting my soul.

14   Jesu who ought to be praised

It were as easy for Jesu
To renew the withered tree
As to wither the new
Were it His will so to do.
    Jesu! Jesu! Jesu!
    Jesu! meet it were to praise Him.

There is no plant in the ground
But is full of His virtue,
There is no form in the strand
But is full of His blessing.

Jesu! Jesu! Jesu!
Jesu! meet it were to praise Him.

There is no life in the sea,
There is no creature in the river,
There is naught in the firmament,
But proclaims His goodness.
Jesu! Jesu! Jesu!
Jesu! meet it were to praise Him.

There is no bird on the wing,
There is no star in the sky,
There is nothing beneath the sun,
But proclaims His goodness.
Jesu! Jesu! Jesu!
Jesu! meet it were to praise Him.

15   The Rock of rocks

On the Rock of rocks,
The peace of Peter and Paul,
Of James and John the beloved,
And of the pure perfect Virgin,
The pure perfect Virgin.

The peace of the Father of joy,
The peace of the Christ of pasch,
The peace of the Spirit of grace,
To ourselves and to our children,
Ourselves and our children.

16   The Lightener of the stars

Behold the Lightener of the stars
On the crests of the clouds,
And the choralists of the sky
    Lauding Him.

Coming down with acclaim
From the Father above,
Harp and lyre of song
    Sounding to Him.

Christ, Thou refuge of my love,
Why should not I raise Thy fame!
Angels and saints melodious
    Singing to Thee.

Thou Son of the Mary of graces,
Of exceeding white purity of beauty,
Joy were it to me to be in the fields
    Of Thy riches.

O Christ my beloved,
O Christ of the Holy Blood,
By day and by night
    I praise Thee.

17   The cross of the saints and the angels

The cross of the saints and of the angels with me
From the top of my face to the edge of my soles.

O Michael mild, O Mary of glory,
O gentle Bride of the locks of gold,
Preserve ye me in the weakly body,
The three preserve me on the just path.
    Oh! three preserve me on the just path.

Preserve ye me in the soul-shrine poor,
Preserve ye me, and I so weak and naked,
Preserve ye me without offence on the way,
The preservation of the three upon me tonight.
  Oh! the three to shield me tonight.

18   The guardian angel

Thou angel of God who hast charge of me
From the dear Father of mercifulness,
The shepherding kind of the fold of the saints
To make round about me this night.

Drive from me every temptation and danger,
Surround me on the sea of unrighteousness,
And in the narrows, crooks, and straits,
Keep thou my coracle, keep it always.

Be thou a bright flame before me,
Be thou a guiding star above me,
Be thou a smooth path below me,
And be a kindly shepherd behind me,
Today, tonight, and for ever.

I am tired and I a stranger,
Lead thou me to the land of angels;
For me it is time to go home
To the court of Christ, to the peace of heaven.

19   Desires

May I speak each day according to Thy justice,
Each day may I show Thy chastening, O God;
May I speak each day according to Thy wisdom,
Each day and night may I be at peace with Thee.

Each day may I count the causes of Thy mercy,
May I each day give heed to Thy laws;
Each day may I compose to Thee a song,
May I harp each day Thy praise, O God.

May I each day give love to Thee, Jesu,
Each night may I do the same;
Each day and night, dark and light,
May I laud Thy goodness to me, O God.

20   Invocation for justice

I will wash my face
In the nine rays of the sun,
As Mary washed her Son
    In the rich fermented milk.

Love be in my countenance,
Benevolence in my mind,
Dew of honey in my tongue,
    My breath as the incense.

Black is yonder town,
Black are those therein,
I am the white swan,
    Queen above them.

I will travel in the name of God,
In likeness of deer, in likeness of horse,
In likeness of serpent, in likeness of king:
    Stronger will it be with me than with all persons.

21   Invocation for justice

God, I am bathing my face
In the nine rays of the sun,
As Mary bathed her Son
    In generous milk fermented.

Sweetness be in my face,
Riches be in my countenance,
Comb-honey be in my tongue,
    My breath as the incense.

Black is yonder house,
Blacker men therein;
I am the white swan,
    Queen over them.

I will go in the name of God,
In likeness of deer, in likeness of horse,
In likeness of serpent, in likeness of king,
    More victorious am I than all persons.

22   Prayer for victory

I bathe my face
In the nine rays of the sun,
As Mary bathed her Son
    In the rich fermented milk.

Honey be in my mouth,
Affection be in my face;
The love that Mary gave her Son
    Be in the heart of all flesh for me.

All-seeing, all-hearing, all-inspiring may God be,
To satisfy and to strengthen me;
Blind, deaf, and dumb, ever, ever be
    My contemners and my mockers.

The tongue of Columba in my head,
The eloquence of Columba in my speech;
The composure of the Victorious Son of grace
    Be mine in presence of the multitude.

23   The lustration

I am bathing my face
In the mild rays of the sun,
As Mary bathed Christ
In the rich milk of Egypt.

Sweetness be in my mouth,
Wisdom be in my speech,
The love the fair Mary gave her Son
Be in the heart of all flesh for me.

The love of Christ in my breast,
The form of Christ protecting me,
There is not in sea nor on land
That can overcome the King of the Lord's Day.

The hand of Bride about my neck,
The hand of Mary about my breast,
The hand of Michael laving me,
The hand of Christ saving me.

24   Bathing prayer

A palmful for thine age,
    A palmful for thy growth,
A palmful for thy throat,
    A flood for thine appetite.

For thy share of the dainty,
    Crowdie and kail;

For thy share of the taking,
   Honey and warm milk.

For thy share of the supping,
   Whisked whey and milk-product;
For thy share of the spoil,
   With bow and with spear.

For thy share of the preparation,
   The yellow eggs of Easter;
For thy share of the treat,
   My treasure and my joy.

For thy share of the feast
   With gifts and with tribute;
For thy share of the treasure,
   Pulset of my love.

For thy share of the chase
Up the face of the Beinn-a-cheo;*
For thy share of the hunting
   And the ruling over hosts.

For thy share of palaces,
In the courts of kings;
For thy share of Paradise
   With its goodness and its peace.

The part of thee that does not grow at dawn,
May it grow at eventide;
The part of thee that does not grow at night,
   May it grow at ridge of middle-day.

   The three palmfuls
   Of the Secret Three,
   To preserve thee
   From every envy,
   Evil eye and death;
   The palmful of the God of Life,

---

*Mount of mist. Probably a particular name and not a general term.

The palmful of the Christ of Love,
The palmful of the Spirit of Peace,
    Triune
    Of Grace.

25 God guide me

God guide me with Thy wisdom,
God chastise me with Thy justice,
God help me with Thy mercy,
God protect me with Thy strength.

God fill me with Thy fullness,
God shield me with Thy shade,
God fill me with Thy grace,
For the sake of Thine Anointed Son.

Jesu Christ of the seed of David,
Visiting One of the Temple,
Sacrificial Lamb of the Garden,
Who died for me.

26 Sleep blessing

Be Thy right hand, O God, under my head,
Be Thy light, O Spirit, over me shining.
And be the cross of the nine angels over me down,
From the crown of my head to the soles of my feet,
    From the crown of my head to the soles of my feet.

O Jesu without offence, crucified cruelly,
Under ban of the wicked Thou wert scourged,
The many evils done of me in the body!
That I cannot this night enumerate,
    That I cannot this night enumerate.

O Thou Ring of the blood of truth,
Cast me not from Thy covenant,
Exact not from me for my transgressions,
Nor omit me in Thy numbering,
    Nor omit me in Thy numbering.

Be the cross of Mary and of Michael over me in peace,
Be my soul dwelling in truth, be my heart free of guile,
Be my soul in peace with thee, Brightness of the
    mountains.
Valiant Michael, meet thou my soul,
    Morn and eve, day and night. May it be so.

27   Come I this day

Come I this day to the Father,
Come I this day to the Son,
Come I to the Holy Spirit powerful;
Come I this day with God,
Come I this day with Christ,
Come I with the Spirit of kindly balm.

God, and Spirit, and Jesus,
From the crown of my head
To the soles of my feet;
Come I with my reputation,
Come I with my testimony,
Come I to Thee, Jesu;
    Jesu, shelter me.

28   The soul plaint

O Jesu! tonight,
Thou Shepherd of the poor,
Thou sinless person
Who didst suffer full sore,
By ban of the wicked,
And wast crucified.

Save me from evil,
Save me from harm,
Save Thou my body,
Sanctify me tonight,
O Jesu! tonight,
Nor leave me.

Endow me with strength,
Thou Herdsman of might,
Guide me aright,
Guide me in Thy strength,
O Jesu! in Thy strength
Preserve me.

29   Sleeping prayer

I am placing my soul and my body
On Thy sanctuary this night, O God,
On Thy sanctuary, O Jesus Christ,
On Thy sanctuary, O Spirit of perfect truth;
    The Three who would defend my cause,
    Nor turn Their backs upon me.

Thou, Father, who art kind and just,
Thou, Son, who didst overcome death,
Thou, Holy Spirit of power,
Be keeping me this night from harm;

The Three who would justify me
Keeping me this night and always.

30   The gifts of the Three

Spirit, give me of Thine abundance,
Father, give me of Thy wisdom,
Son, give me in my need,
      Jesus beneath the shelter of Thy shield.

I lie down tonight,
With the Triune of my strength,
With the Father, with Jesus,
      With the Spirit of might.

31   Sleep prayer

O Jesu without sin,
King of the poor,
Who wert sorely subdued
Under ban of the wicked,
Shield Thou me this night
      From Judas.

My soul on Thine own arm, O Christ,
Thou the King of the City of Heaven,
Thou it was who bought'st my soul, O Jesu,
      Thou it was who didst sacrifice Thy life for me.

Protect Thou me because of my sorrow,
For the sake of Thy passion, Thy wounds, and Thine own
      blood,
And take me in safety tonight
      Near to the City of God.

32   Resting blessing

In name of the Lord Jesus,
And of the Spirit of healing balm,
In name of the Father of Israel,
    I lay me down to rest.

If there be evil threat or quirk,
Or covert act intent on me,
God free me and encompass me,
    And drive from me mine enemy.

In name of the Father precious,
And of the Spirit of healing balm,
In name of the Lord Jesus,
    I lay me down to rest.

God, help me and encompass me,
From this hour till the hour of my death.

33   Sleep consecration

I lie down tonight
With fair Mary and with her Son,
With pure-white Michael,
And with Bride beneath her mantle.

I lie down with God,
And God will lie down with me,
I will not lie down with Satan,
Nor shall Satan lie down with me.

O God of the poor,
Help me this night,
Omit me not entirely
From Thy treasure-house.

For the many wounds
That I inflicted on Thee,

I cannot this night
Enumerate them.

Thou King of the blood of truth,
Do not forget me in Thy dwelling-place,
Do not exact from me for my transgressions,
Do not omit me in Thine ingathering,
    In Thine ingathering.

34   Bed blessing

I am lying down tonight as beseems
In the fellowship of Christ, son of the Virgin of ringlets.
In the fellowship of the gracious Father of glory,
In the fellowship of the Spirit of powerful aid.

I am lying down tonight with God,
And God tonight will lie down with me,
I will not lie down tonight with sin, nor shall
Sin nor sin's shadow lie down with me.

I am lying down tonight with the Holy Spirit,
And the Holy Spirit this night will lie down with me,
I will lie down this night with the Three of my love,
And the Three of my love will lie down with me.

35   The sleep prayer

I am now going into the sleep,
Be it that I in health shall waken;
If death be to me in the death-sleep,
Be it that on Thine own arm,
O God of Grace, I in peace shall waken;
Be it on Thine own beloved arm,
O God of Grace, that I in peace shall waken.

Be my soul on Thy right hand, O God,
Thou King of the heaven of heavens;
Thou it was who bought'st me with Thy blood,
Thou it was who gavest Thy life for me,
Encompass Thou me this night, O God,
That no harm, no evil shall me befall.

Whilst the body is dwelling in the sleep,
The soul is soaring in the shadow of heaven,
Be the red-white Michael meeting the soul,
Early and late, night and day,
Early and late, night and day.
    Amen.

36 Sleep consecration

I am lying down tonight,
With Father, with Son,
With the Spirit of Truth,
Who shield me from harm.

I will not lie with evil,
Nor shall evil lie with me,
But I will lie down with God,
And God will lie down with me.

God and Christ and Spirit Holy,
And the cross of the nine white angels,
Be protecting me as Three and as One,
From the top tablet of my face to the soles of my feet.

Thou King of the sun and of glory,
Thou Jesu, Son of the Virgin fragrant,
Keep Thou us from the glen of tears,
And from the house of grief and gloom,
    Keep us from the glen of tears,
    From the house of grief and gloom.

37   Bed blessing

I am lying down tonight,
With Mary mild and with her Son,
With the Mother of my King,
Who is shielding me from harm.

I will not lie down with evil,
Nor shall evil lie down with me,
But I will lie down with God,
And God will lie down with me.

God and Mary and Michael kindly
And the cross of the nine angels fair,
Be shielding me as Three and as One,
From the brow of my face to the edge of my soles.

I beseech Peter, I beseech Paul,
I beseech Mary, I beseech the Son,
I beseech the trustful Apostles twelve
To preserve me from hurt and harm;
        O from dying tonight,
        From dying tonight!

O God! O Mary of Glory!
O Jesu! Son of the Virgin fragrant,
Sain Ye us from the pains everlasting,
And from the fire fierce and murky,
        From the pains everlasting,
        And from the fire fierce and murky!

38   The soul shrine

God, give charge to Thy blessed angels,
        To keep guard around this stead tonight,
A band sacred, strong, and steadfast,
        That will shield this soul-shrine from harm.

Safeguard Thou, God, this household tonight,
  Themselves and their means and their fame,
Deliver them from death, from distress, from harm,
  From the fruits of envy and of enmity.

Give Thou to us, O God of peace,
  Thankfulness despite our loss,
To obey Thy statutes here below,
  And to enjoy Thyself above.

39   Soul-shrine

Thou angel of God who hast charge of me
From the fragrant Father of mercifulness,
The gentle encompassing of the Sacred Heart
To make round my soul-shrine this night,
  Oh, round my soul-shrine this night.

Ward from me every distress and danger,
Encompass my course over the ocean of truth,
I pray thee, place thy pure light before me,
O bright beauteous angel on this very night,
  Bright beauteous angel on this very night.

Be Thyself the guiding star above me,
Illume Thou to me every reef and shoal,
Pilot my barque on the crest of the wave,
To the restful haven of the waveless sea,
  Oh, the restful haven of the waveless sea.

40   I lie in my bed

I lie in my bed
As I would lie in the grave,
Thine arm beneath my neck,
    Thou Son of Mary victorious.

Angels shall watch me
And I lying in slumber,
And angels shall guard me
    In the sleep of the grave.

Uriel shall be at my feet,
Ariel shall be at my back,
Gabriel shall be at my head,
    And Raphael shall be at my side.

Michael shall be with my soul,
The strong shield of my love!
And the Physician Son of Mary
Shall put the salve to mine eye,
    The Physician Son of Mary
    Shall put the salve to mine eye!

41   Morning prayer

Thanks be to Thee, Jesus Christ,
Who brought'st me up from last night,
To the gladsome light of this day,
To win everlasting life for my soul,
Through the blood Thou didst shed for me.

Praise be to Thee, O God, for ever,
For the blessings Thou didst bestow on me:
My food, my speech, my work, my health.

And I beseech Thee
To shield me from sin,

To shield me from ill,
To sain me this night,
And I low and poor,
O God of the poor!
O Christ of the wounds!
Give me wisdom along with Thy grace.

May the Holy One claim me,
And protect me on sea and on land,
And lead me on from step to step,
To the peace of the Everlasting City,
      The peace of the Everlasting City!

42   The dedication

Thanks to Thee, God,
Who brought'st me from yesterday
To the beginning of today,
Everlasting joy
To earn for my soul
With good intent.
And for every gift of peace
Thou bestowest on me,
My thoughts, my words,
My deeds, my desires
I dedicate to Thee.
I supplicate Thee,
I beseech Thee,
To keep me from offence,
And to shield me tonight,
For the sake of Thy wounds
With Thine offering of grace.

43   A resting prayer

God shield the house, the fire, the kine,
Every one who dwells herein tonight.
Shield myself and my beloved group,
Preserve us from violence and from harm;
Preserve us from foes this night,
For the sake of the Son of the Mary Mother,
In this place, and in every place wherein they dwell
    tonight,
On this night and on every night,
    This night and every night.

44   House protecting

God, bless the world and all that is therein.
God, bless my spouse and my children,
God, bless the eye that is in my head,
And bless, O God, the handling of my hand;
What time I rise in the morning early,
What time I lie down late in bed;
    Bless my rising in the morning early,
    And my lying down late in bed.

God, protect the house, and the household,
God, consecrate the children of the motherhood,
God, encompass the flocks and the young;
Be Thou after them and tending them,
What time the flocks ascend hill and wold,
What time I lie down to sleep;
    What time the flocks ascend hill and wold,
    What time I lie down in peace to sleep.

45   Blessing of house

God bless the house,
From site to stay,
From beam to wall,
From end to end,
From ridge to basement,
From balk to roof-tree,
From found to summit,
    Found and summit.

46   To whom shall I offer oblation

To whom shall I offer oblation
In name of Michael on high?
I will give tithe of my means
To the forsaken illustrious One.

Because of all that I have seen,
Of His peace and of His mercy,
Lift Thou my soul to Thee, O Son of God,
Nor leave me ever.

Remember me in the mountain,
Under Thy wing shield Thou me;
Rock of truth, do not forsake me,
My wish it were ever to be near Thee.

Give to me the wedding garment,
Be angels conversing with me in every need,
Be the holy apostles protecting me,
The fair Mary and Thou, Jesu of grace,
    The fair Mary and Thou, Jesu of grace.

47 Hail, Mary

Hail, Mary! hail, Mary!
    Queen of grace, Mother of mercy;
Hail, Mary, in manner surpassing,
    Fount of our health, source of our joy.

To thee we, night and day,
    Erring children of Adam and Eve,
Lift our voice in supplication,
    In groans and grief and tears.

Bestow upon us, thou Root of gladness,
    Since thou art the cup of generous graces,
The faith of John, and Peter, and Paul,
    With the wings of Ariel on the heights of the clouds.

Vouchsafe to us, thou golden branch,
    A mansion in the Realm of peace,
Rest from the perils and stress of waves,
    Beneath the shade of the fruit of thy womb, Jesu.

48 Hail to thee, Mary

Hail to thee, Mary, Mother!
Thou art full of loving grace,
The Lord God is always with thee,
Blessed art thou Mary among women,
Blessed is the fruit of thy womb, Jesus,
Blessed art thou, Queen of grace;
Thou holy Mary, thou Mother of Jesus,
Plead for me a miserable sinner,
Now and at the hour of death,
    Now and at the hour of death.

49   The battle to come

Jesus, Thou Son of Mary, I call on Thy name,
And on the name of John the apostle beloved,
And on the names of all the saints in the red domain,
To shield me in the battle to come,
    To shield me in the battle to come.

When the mouth shall be closed,
When the eye shall be shut,
When the breath shall cease to rattle,
When the heart shall cease to throb,
    When the heart shall cease to throb.

When the Judge shall take the throne,
And when the cause is fully pleaded,
O Jesu, Son of Mary, shield Thou my soul,
O Michael fair, acknowledge my departure.
    O Jesu, Son of Mary, shield Thou my soul!
    O Michael fair, receive my departure!

50   The baptism blessing

Thou Being who inhabitest the heights
Imprint Thy blessing betimes,
Remember Thou the child of my body,
In Name of the Father of peace;
When the priest of the King
On him puts the water of meaning,
Grant him the blessing of the Three
    Who fill the heights.
The blessing of the Three
    Who fill the heights.

Sprinkle down upon him Thy grace,
Give Thou to him virtue and growth,
Give Thou to him strength and guidance,

Give Thou to him flocks and possessions,
Sense and reason void of guile,
Angel wisdom in his day,
That he may stand without reproach
    In Thy presence.
He may stand without reproach
    In Thy presence.

51   The soul leading

Be this soul on Thine arm, O Christ,
Thou King of the City of Heaven.
    Amen.

Since Thou, O Christ, it was who bought'st this soul,
Be its peace on Thine own keeping.
    Amen.

And may the strong Michael, high king of the angels,
Be preparing the path before this soul, O God.
    Amen.

Oh! the strong Michael in peace with thee, soul,
And preparing for thee the way to the kingdom
    of the Son of God.
    Amen.

52   The death blessing

God, omit not this woman from Thy covenant,
And the many evils which she in the body committed,
That she cannot this night enumerate.
The many evils that she in the body committed,
That she cannot this night enumerate.

Be this soul on Thine own arm, O Christ,
Thou King of the City of Heaven,
And since Thine it was, O Christ, to buy the soul,
At the time of the balancing of the beam,
At the time of the bringing in the judgment,
Be it now on Thine own right hand,
Oh! on Thine own right hand.

And be the holy Michael, king of angels,
Coming to meet the soul,
And leading it home
To the heaven of the Son of God.
> The Holy Michael, high king of angels,
> Coming to meet the soul,
> And leading it home
> To the heaven of the Son of God.

53 Soul peace

Since Thou Christ it was who didst buy the soul—
At the time of yielding the life,
At the time of pouring the sweat,
At the time of offering the clay,
At the time of shedding the blood,
At the time of balancing the beam,
At the time of severing the breath,
At the time of delivering the judgment,
Be its peace upon Thine own ingathering;
Jesus Christ Son of gentle Mary,
Be its peace upon Thine own ingathering,
> O Jesus! upon Thine own ingathering.

And may Michael white kindly,
High king of the holy angels,
Take possession of the beloved soul,
And shield it home to the Three of surpassing love,
> Oh! to the Three of surpassing love.

54   The new moon

In name of the Holy Spirit of grace,
In name of the Father of the City of peace,
In name of Jesus who took death off us,
Oh! in name of the Three who shield us in every need,
If well thou hast found us tonight,
Seven times better mayest thou leave us without harm,
Thou bright white Moon of the seasons,
Bright white Moon of the seasons.

Seasons

55 Christmas hail

Hail to the King, hail to the King,
Blessed is He, blessed is He,
Hail to the King, hail to the King,
Blessed is He who has come betimes,
Hail to the King, hail to the King,
Blessed be the house and all therein,
Hail to the King, hail to the King,
'Twixt stock and stone and stave,
Hail to the King, hail to the King,
Consign it to God from corslet to cover,
Be the health of men therein,
Hail to the King, hail to the King,
Blessed is He, blessed is He,
Hail to the King, hail to the King,
Blessed is He, blessed is He,
Hail to the King, hail to the King,
Lasting round the house be ye,
Hail to the King, hail to the King,

37

Healthy round the hearth be ye,
    Hail to the King, hail to the King,
Many be the stakes in the house,
And men dwelling on the foundation,
    Hail to the King, hail to the King,
Blessed is He, blessed is He,
    Hail to the King, hail to the King,
Blessed is He, blessed is He.

    Hail to the King, hail to the King,
This night is the eve of the great Nativity,
    Hail to the King, hail to the King,
Blessed is He, blessed is He,
    Hail to the King, hail to the King,
Born is the Son of Mary the Virgin,
    Hail to the King, hail to the King,
Blessed is He, blessed is He,
    Hail to the King, hail to the King,
The soles of His feet have reached the earth,
    Hail to the King, hail to the King,
Blessed is He, blessed is He,
    Hail to the King, hail to the King,
Illumined the sun the mountains high,
    Hail to the King, hail to the King,
Blessed is He, blessed is He.
Shone the earth, shone the land,
    Hail to the King, hail to the King,
Blessed is He, blessed is He,
    Hail to the King, hail to the King,
Heard was the wave upon the strand,
    Hail to the King, hail to the King,
Blessed is He, blessed is He,
Blessed is He, blessed is He,
    Hail to the King, hail to the King,
Blessed the King,
Without beginning, without end,
To everlasting, to eternity,
To all ages, to all time.

56   Christmas carol

Hail King! hail King! blessed is He! blessed is He!
Hail King! hail King! blessed is He! blessed is He!
Hail King! hail King! blessed is He, the King, of whom
    we sing,
        All hail! let there be joy!

This night is the eve of the great Nativity,
Born is the Son of Mary the Virgin,
The soles of His feet have reached the earth,
The Son of glory down from on high,
Heaven and earth glowed to Him,
        All hail! let there be joy!

The peace of earth to Him, the joy of heaven to Him,
Behold His feet have reached the world;
The homage of a King be His, the welcome of a Lamb
    be His,
King all victorious, Lamb all glorious,
Earth and ocean illumed to Him,
        All hail! let there be joy!

The mountains glowed to Him, the plains glowed to Him,
The voice of the waves with the song of the strand,
Announcing to us that Christ is born,
Son of the King of kings from the land of salvation;
Shone the sun on the mountains high to Him,
        All hail! let there be joy!

Shone to Him the earth and sphere together,
God the Lord has opened a Door;
Son of Mary Virgin, hasten Thou to help me,
Thou Christ of hope, Thou Door of joy,
Golden Sun of hill and mountain,
        All hail! let there be joy!

57   Christmas chant

Hail King! hail King! blessed is He! blessed is He!
Hail King! hail King! blessed is He! blessed is He!
    Ho, hail! blessed the King!
    Ho, hi! let there be joy!

Prosperity be upon this dwelling,
On all that ye have heard and seen,
On the bare bright floor flags,
On the shapely standing stone staves,
    Hail King! hail King! blessed is He! blessed is He!

Bless this house and all that it contains,
From rafter and stone and beam;
Deliver it to God from pall to cover,
Be the healing of men therein,
    Hail King! hail King! blessed is He! blessed is He!

Be ye in lasting possession of the house,
Be ye healthy about the hearth;
Many be the ties and stakes in the homestead,
People dwelling on this foundation,
    Hail King! hail King! blessed is He! blessed is He!

Offer to the Being from found to cover,
Include stave and stone and beam;
Offer again both rods and cloth,
Be health to the people therein,
    Hail King! hail King! blessed is He! blessed is He!
    Hail King! hail King! blessed is He! blessed is He!
    Ho, hail! blessed the King!
    Let there be joy!

Blessed the King,
Without beginning, without ending,
To everlasting, to eternity,
Every generation for aye,
Ho! hi! let there be joy!

58   Hey the Gift

Hey the Gift, ho the Gift,
Hey the Gift on the living.

The fair Mary went upon her knee,
It was the King of glory who was on her breast.

The side of the sack, the side of the sark,
The hide is struck upon the spar

To tell to us that Christ is born,
The King of kings of the land of salvation.

I see the hills, I see the strand,
I see the host upon the wing.

I see angels on clouds,
Coming with speech and friendship to us.

59   Hey the Gift, ho the Gift

Hey the Gift, ho the Gift,
Hey the Gift on the living.

Son of the dawn, Son of the clouds,
Son of the planet, Son of the star,
    Hey the Gift, etc.

Son of the rain, Son of the dew,
Son of the welkin, Son of the sky,
    Hey the Gift, etc.

Son of the flame, Son of the light,
Son of the sphere, Son of the globe,
    Hey the Gift, etc.

Son of the elements, Son of the heavens,
Son of the moon, Son of the sun,
    Hey the Gift, etc.

Son of Mary of the God-mind,
And the Son of God first of all news,
  Hey the Gift, etc.

60 The Gift of power

I am the Gift, I am the Poor,
I am the Man of this night.

I am the Son of God in the door,
On Monday seeking the gifts.

Noble is Bride the gentle fair on her knee,
Noble the King of glory on her breast.

Son of the moon, Son of the sun,
Great Son of Mary of God-like mind.

A cross on each right shoulder,
I am in the door, open thou.

I see the hills, I see the strand,
I see angels heralding on high.

I see the dove shapely, benign,
Coming with kindness and friendship to us.

61 The Virgin and child

Behold the Virgin approaching,
Christ so young on her breast.

O Mary Virgin! and O Holy Son!
Bless ye the house and all therein.

Bless ye the food, bless ye the board,
Bless ye the corn, the flock and the store.

What time to us the quarter was scarce,
It is thou thyself, Virgin, who wast mother to us.

Thou art brighter than the waxing moon
Rising over the mountains.

Thou art brighter than the summer sun,
Under his fullness of joy.

Since the bard must not tarry,
Place ye alms in the bag with a blessing.

Servant am I of God the Son on the threshold,
For the sake of God, arise thyself and open to me.

62   The Shepherd of the Flock was born

That night the star shone
Was born the Shepherd of the Flock,
Of the Virgin of the hundred charms,
 The Mary Mother.

The Trinity eternal by her side,
In the manger cold and lowly.
Come and give tithes of thy means
 To the Healing Man.

The foam-white breastling beloved,
Without one home in the world,
The tender holy Babe forth driven,
 Immanuel!

Ye three angels of power,
Come ye, come ye down;
To the Christ of the people
 Give ye salutation.

Kiss ye His hands,
Dry ye His feet
With the hair of your heads;

And O! Thou world-pervading God,
And Ye, Jesu, Michael, Mary,
   Do not Ye forsake us.

63   Hogmanay of the sack

Hogmanay of the sack,
Hogmanay of the sack,
   Strike the hide,
   Strike the hide.
Hogmanay of the sack,
Hogmanay of the sack,
   Beat the skin,
   Beat the skin.
Hogmanay of the sack,
Hogmanay of the sack,
   Down with it! up with it!
   Strike the hide.
Hogmanay of the sack,
Hogmanay of the sack,
   Down with it! up with it!
   Beat the skin.
Hogmanay of the sack,
Hogmanay of the sack.

64   Hogmanay carol

I am now come to your country,
To renew to you the Hogmanay,
I need not tell you of it,
It was in the time of our forefathers.

I ascend by the door lintel,
I descend by the doorstep,

I will sing my song becomingly,
Mannerly, slowly, mindfully.

The Hogmanay skin is in my pocket,
Great will be the smoke from it presently.
The house-man will get it in his hand,
He will place its nose in the fire;
He will go sunwards round the babes,
And for seven verities round the housewife.

The housewife it is she who deserves it,
The hand to dispense to us the Hogmanay,
A small gift of the bloom of summer,
Much I wish it with the bread.

Give it to us if it be possible,
If you may not, do not detain us;
I am the servant of God's Son at the door,
Arise thyself and open to me.

65   The song of Hogmanay

Now since we came to the country
To renew to you the Hogmanay,
Time will not allow us to explain,
    It has been since the age of our fathers.

Ascending the wall of the house,
Descending at the door,
My carol to say modestly,
    As becomes me at the Hogmanay.

The Hogmanay skin is in my pocket,
Great the fume that will come from that;
No one who shall inhale its odour,
    But shall be for ever from it healthy.

The house-man will get it in his grasp,
He will put its point in the fire;

He will go sunwise round the children,
    And very specially round the goodwife.

The wife will get it, she it is who deserves it,
The hand to distribute the Hogmanay,
The hand to bestow upon us cheese and butter,
    The hand without niggardliness, without meanness.

Since drought has come upon the land,
And that we do not expect rarity,
A little of the substance of the summer,
    Would we desire with the bread.

If that we are not to have it,
If thou mayest, do not detain us;
I am the servant of God's Son on Hogmanay,
    Arise thyself and open the door.
    Hogmanay here! Hogmanay here!

66 Hogmanay

We are come to the door,
To see if we be the better of our visit,
To tell the generous women of the townland
That tomorrow is Calendae Day.

After being entertained the guisers go sunwise round the fire singing:

May God bless the dwelling,
Each stone, and beam, and stave,
All food, and drink, and clothing,
May health of men he always there.

Should the guisers be inhospitably treated, they file round the fire wither-shins and walk out, and raise a cairn in or near the door, called carnan mollachd (cairn of malison), carnan cronachd (scathe, or evil, cairn).

    They tramp loudly, shaking the dust of the place off their feet, and intoning with a deep voice the following and other maledictions:

The malison of God and of Hogmanay be on you,
And the scathe of the plaintive buzzard,
Of the hen-harrier, of the raven, of the eagle,
And the scathe of the sneaking fox.

The scathe of the dog and of the cat be on you,
Of the boar, of the badger, and of the *brugha,*
Of the hipped bear and of the wild wolf,
And the scathe of the foul foumart.

67   The blessing of the New Year

God, bless to me the new day,
Never vouchsafed to me before;
It is to bless Thine own presence
Thou hast given me this time, O God.

Bless Thou to me mine eye,
May mine eye bless all it sees;
I will bless my neighbour,
May my neighbour bless me.
God, give me a clean heart,
Let me not from sight of Thine eye;
Bless to me my children and my wife,
And bless to me my means and my cattle.

68   Christ the Priest above us

Christ the Priest above us,
Ordained of God for all living.
    Christ the Priest above us.

Tonight, the night of the cross of agony,
The cross of anguish to which Christ was crucified.
    Christ the Priest above us.

Noble the Gift! noble the Poor!
Noble the Man of this night.
  Christ the Priest above us.

It was Bride the fair who went on her knee,
It is the King of glory who is in her lap.
  Christ the Priest above us.

I hear the hills, I hear the seas,
I hear the angels heralding to earth
  Christ the Priest above us.

I hear Cairbre of the shapely, rounded limbs,
Coming softly in friendship to us.
  Christ the Priest above us.

Great the assemblage upon this knoll,
Without the envy of man to another.
  Christ the Priest above us.

I am servant of God the Son at the door,
Oh! arise thou thyself and open to me.
  Christ the Priest above us.

69 The day of St. Columba

Thursday of Columba benign,
Day to send sheep on prosperity,
Day to send cow on calf,
Day to put the web in the warp.

Day to put coracle on the brine,
Day to place the staff to the flag,
Day to bear, day to die,
Day to hunt the heights.

Day to put horses in harness,
Day to send herds to pasture,
Day to make prayer efficacious,

Day of my beloved, the Thursday,
   Day of my beloved, the Thursday.

70 Genealogy of Bride

The genealogy of the holy maiden Bride,
Radiant flame of gold, noble foster-mother of Christ.
Bride the daughter of Dugall the brown,
Son of Aodh, son of Art, son of Conn,
Son of Crearar, son of Cis, son of Carmac, son of Carruin.

Every day and every night
That I say the genealogy of Bride,
I shall not be killed, I shall not be harried,
I shall not be put in cell, I shall not be wounded,
Neither shall Christ leave me in forgetfulness.

No fire, no sun, no moon shall burn me,
No lake, no water, nor sea shall drown me,
No arrow of fairy nor dart of fay shall wound me,
And I under the protection of my Holy Mary,
And my gentle foster-mother is my beloved Bride.

71 Bride the aid-woman

There came to me assistance,
Mary fair and Bride;
As Anna bore Mary,
As Mary bore Christ,
As Eile bore John the Baptist
Without flaw in him,
Aid thou me in mine unbearing,
   Aid me, O Bride!

As Christ was conceived of Mary
Full perfect on every hand,
Assist thou me, foster-mother,
The conception to bring from the bone;
And as thou didst aid the Virgin of joy,
Without gold, without corn, without kine,
Aid thou me, great is my sickness,
    Aid me, O Bride!

72 Magnus of my love

O Magnus of my love,
Thou it is who would'st us guide.
Thou fragrant body of grace,
    Remember us.

Remember us, thou Saint of power,
Who didst encompass and protect the people,
Succour thou us in our distress,
    Nor forsake us.

Lift our flocks to the hills,
Quell the wolf and the fox,
Ward from us spectre, giant, fury,
    And oppression.

Surround cows and herds,
Surround sheep and lambs;
Keep from them the water-vole,
    And the field-vole.

Sprinkle dew from the sky upon kine,
Give growth to grass, and corn, and sap to plants,
Watercress, deer's-grass, *ceis,* burdock,
    And daisy.

O Magnus of fame,
On the barque of the heroes,

On the crests of the waves,
On the sea, on the land,
    Aid and preserve us.

73 The Beltane blessing

Bless, O Threefold true and bountiful,
Myself, my spouse, and my children,
My tender children and their beloved mother at their head.
On the fragrant plain, on the gay mountain sheiling,
    On the fragrant plain, on the gay mountain sheiling.

Everything within my dwelling or in my possession,
All kine and crops, all flocks and corn,
From Hallow Eve to Beltane Eve,
With goodly progress and gentle blessing,
From sea to sea, and every river mouth,
    From wave to wave, and base of waterfall.

Be the Three Persons taking possession of all to me
    belonging,
Be the sure Trinity protecting me in truth;
Oh! satisfy my soul in the words of Paul,
And shield my loved ones beneath the wing of Thy glory,
    Shield my loved ones beneath the wing of Thy glory.

Bless everything and every one,
Of this little household by my side;
Place the cross of Christ on us with the power of love,
Till we see the land of joy,
    Till we see the land of joy.

What time the kine shall forsake the stalls,
What time the sheep shall forsake the folds,
What time the goats shall ascend to the mount of mist,
May the tending of the Triune follow them,
    May the tending of the Triune follow them.

Thou Being who didst create me at the beginning,
Listen and attend me as I bend the knee to Thee,
Morning and evening as is becoming in me,
In Thine own presence, O God of life,
    In Thine own presence, O God of life.

74   The Beltane blessing

Mary, thou mother of saints,
Bless our flocks and bearing kine;
Hate nor scathe let not come near us,
Drive from us the ways of the wicked.

Keep thine eye every Monday and Tuesday
On the bearing kine and the pairing queys;
Accompany us from hill to sea,
Gather thyself the sheep and their progeny.

Every Wednesday and Thursday be with them,
Be thy gracious hand always about them;
Tend the cows down to their stalls,
Tend the sheep down to their folds!

Every Friday be thou, O Saint, at their head,
Lead the sheep from the face of the bens,
With their innocent little lambs following them,
Encompass them with God's encompassing.

Every Saturday be likewise with them,
Bring the goats in with their young,
Every kid and goat to the sea side,
And from the Rock of Aegir on high,
With cresses green about its summit.

The strength of the Triune be our shield in distress,
The strength of Christ, His peace and His Pasch,
The strength of the Spirit, Physician of health,
And of the precious Father the King of grace;

And of [saint];
And of [saint];
And of every other saint who succeeded them
And who earned the repose of the kingdom of God.

Bless ourselves and our children,
Bless every one who shall come from our loins,
Bless him whose name we bear,
Bless, O God, her from whose womb we came.

Every holiness, blessing, and power,
Be yielded to us every time and every hour,
In name of the Holy Threefold above,
Father, Son, and Spirit everlasting.

Be the Cross of Christ to shield us downward,
Be the Cross of Christ to shield us upward,
Be the Cross of Christ to shield us roundward,
Accepting our Beltane blessing from us,
    Accepting our Beltane blessing from us.

75   Hymn of the procession

Valiant Michael of the white steeds,
Who subdued the Dragon of blood,
For love of God, for pains of Mary's Son,
Spread thy wing over us, shield us all,
    Spread thy wing over us, shield us all.

Mary beloved! Mother of the White Lamb,
Shield, oh shield us, pure Virgin of nobleness,
And Bride the beauteous, shepherdess of the flocks.
Safeguard thou our cattle, surround us together,
    Safeguard thou our cattle, surround us together.

And Columba, beneficent, benign,
In name of Father, and of Son, and of Spirit Holy,
Through the Three-in-one, through the Trinity,

Encompass thou ourselves, shield our procession,
    Encompass thou ourselves, shield our procession.

O Father! O Son! O Spirit Holy!
Be the Triune with us day and night,
On the machair plain or on the mountain ridge
Be the Triune with us and His arm around our head,
    Be the Triune with us and His arm around our head.

Barra fishermen
O Father! O Son! O Spirit Holy!
Be thou, Three-One, with us day and night,
And on the back of the wave as on the mountain side
Our Mother shall be with us with her arm under our head.
    And on the back of the wave as on the mountain side
    Our Mother shall be with us with her arm under
      our head.

76 The feast day of Mary

On the feast day of Mary the fragrant,
Mother of the Shepherd of the flocks,
I cut me a handful of the new corn,
I dried it gently in the sun,
I rubbed it sharply from the husk
    With mine own palms.

I ground it in a quern on Friday,
I baked it on a fan of sheepskin,
I toasted it to a fire of rowan,
And I shared it round my people.

I went sunways round my dwelling,
In name of the Mary Mother,
Who promised to preserve me,
Who did preserve me,
And who will preserve me,

In peace, in flocks,
In righteousness of heart,
In labour, in love,
In wisdom, in mercy,
For the sake of Thy Passion.
Thou Christ of grace
Who till the day of my death
Wilt never forsake me!
 Oh, till the day of my death
 Wilt never forsake me!

77 Michael the victorious

Thou Michael the victorious,
I make my circuit under thy shield,
Thou Michael of the white steed,
And of the bright brilliant blades,
Conqueror of the dragon,
Be thou at my back,
Thou ranger of the heavens,
Thou warrior of the King of all,
 O Michael the victorious,
 My pride and my guide,
 O Michael the victorious,
 The glory of mine eye.

I make my circuit
In the fellowship of my saint,
On the machair, on the meadow,
On the cold heathery hill;
Though I should travel ocean
And the hard globe of the world
No harm can ever befall me
'Neath the shelter of thy shield;
 O Michael the victorious,
 Jewel of my heart,

O Michael the victorious,
God's shepherd thou art.

Be the sacred Three of Glory
Aye at peace with me,
With my horses, with my cattle,
With my woolly sheep in flocks.
With the crops growing in the field
Or ripening in the sheaf,
On the machair, on the moor,
In cole, in heap, or stack.
Every thing on high or low,
Every furnishing and flock,
Belong to the holy Triune of glory,
And to Michael the victorious.

78   The blessing of the *struan*

Each meal beneath my roof,
They will all be mixed together,
In name of God the Son,
Who gave them growth.

Milk, and eggs, and butter,
The good produce of our own flock,
There shall be no dearth in our land,
Nor in our dwelling.

In name of Michael of my love,
Who bequeathed to us the power,
With the blessing of the Lamb,
And of His Mother.

Humble us at thy footstool,
Be thine own sanctuary around us,
Ward from us spectre, sprite, oppression,
And preserve us.

Consecrate the produce of our land,
Bestow prosperity and peace,
In name of the Father the King,
    And of the three beloved apostles.

Dandelion, smooth garlic,
Foxglove, woad, and butterwort,
The three carle-doddies,
    And marigold.

Gray *cailpeach* plucked,
The seven-pronged seven times,
The mountain yew, ruddy heath,
    And madder.

I will put water on them all,
In precious name of the Son of God,
In name of Mary the generous,
    And of Patrick.

When we shall sit down
To take our food,
I will sprinkle in the name of God
    On the children.

79 The poem of the Lord's Day

The poem of the Lord's Day, O bright God,
Truth under the strength of Christ always.

On the Lord's Day Mary was born,
Mother of Christ of golden yellow hair,
On the Lord's Day Christ was born
    As an honour to men.

The Lord's Day, the seventh day,
God ordained to take rest,
To keep the life everlasting,
Without taking use of ox or man,

Or of creature as Mary desired,
Without spinning thread of silk or of satin,
Without sewing, without embroidery either,
Without sowing, without harrowing, without reaping,
Without rowing, without games, without fishing,
Without going out to the hunting hill,
Without trimming arrows on the Lord's Day,
Without cleaning byre, without threshing corn,
Without kiln, without mill on the Lord's Day.

Whosoever would keep the Lord's Day,
Even would it be to him and lasting,
From setting of sun on Saturday
Till rising of sun on Monday.

He would obtain recompense therefrom,
Produce after the ploughs,
Fish on the pure salt-water stream,
Fish excelling in every river confluence.

The water of the Lord's Day mild as honey,
Whoso would partake of it as drink
Would obtain health in consequence
From every disease afflicting him.

The weeping of the Lord's Day is out of place,
A woman doing it is untimely;
Let her weep betimes on Monday,
But not weep once on the Lord's Day.

The wood of the Lord's Day is too soon.
In the pool it is pitiful,
Though its head should fall in char,
It would till Monday be dormant.
About noon on the Monday,
The wood will arise very quickly,
And by the great flood without
Hasten the story of my trouble.
Without any searching for lamb, sheep, kid or goat
That would not belong to the King in the cause.

It is now it ought to be burnt,
Without listening to the clamour of the stranger,
Nor to the blind babbling of the public.

To keep corn on a high hillock,
To bring physician to a violent disease,
To send a cow to the potent bull of the herd,
To go with a beast to a cattle-fold,
Far or near be the distance,
Every creature needs attention.
To allow a boat under her sail from land,
From land to the country of her unacquaintance.

Whoso would meditate my lay,
And say it every Monday eve,
The luck of Michael would be on his head,
And never would he see perdition.

80 Hymn of the Sunday

On the holy Sunday of thy God
Give thou thine heart to all mankind,
To thy father and thy mother loving,
Beyond any person or thing in the world.

Do not covet large or small,
Do not despise weakling or poor,
Semblance of evil allow not near thee,
Never give nor earn thou shame.

The ten commands God gave thee,
Understand them early and prove,
Believe direct in the King of the elements,
Put behind thee ikon-worship.

Be faithful to thine overlord,
Be true to thy king in every need,

Be true to thine own self besides,
True to thy High King above all obstacles.

Do not thou malign any man,
Lest thou thyself maligned shouldst be,
And shouldst thou travel ocean and earth,
Follow the very step of God's Anointed.

81   Poem of the flood

On Monday will come the great storm
Which the airy firmament will pour,
We shall be obedient the while,
        All who will hearken.

On Tuesday will come the other element,
Heart paining, hard piercing,
Wringing from pure pale cheeks
        Blood, like showers of wine.

On Wednesday will blow the wind,
Sweeping bare strath and plain,
Showering gusts of galling grief,
        Thunder bursts and rending hills.

On Thursday will pour the shower,
Driving people into blind flight,
Faster than the foliage on the trees,
        Like the leaves of Mary's plant in terror trembling.

On Friday will come the dool cloud of darkness,
The direst dread that ever came over the world,
Leaving multitudes bereft of reason,
        Grass and fish beneath the same flagstone.

On Saturday will come the great sea,
Rushing like a mighty river;
All will be at their best
        Hastening to a hill of safety.

On Sunday will arise my King,
Full of ire and tribulation,
Listening to the bitter talk of each man,
    A red cross on each right shoulder.

Labour

82 Blessing of the kindling

I will kindle my fire this morning
In presence of the holy angels of heaven,
In presence of Ariel of the loveliest form,
In presence of Uriel of the myriad charms,
Without malice, without jealousy, without envy,
Without fear, without terror of any one under the sun,
But the Holy Son of God to shield me.
  Without malice, without jealousy, without envy,
  Without fear, without terror of any one under
    the sun
  But the Holy Son of God to shield me.

God, kindle Thou in my heart within
A flame of love to my neighbour,
To my foe, to my friend, to my kindred all,
To the brave, to the knave, to the thrall,
O Son of the loveliest Mary,
From the lowliest thing that liveth,
To the Name that is highest of all.
  O Son of the loveliest Mary,
  From the lowliest thing that liveth,
  To the Name that is highest of all.

83 Kindling the fire

I will raise the hearth-fire
As Mary would.
The encirclement of Bride and of Mary
On the fire, and on the floor,
And on the household all.

Who are they on the bare floor?
John and Peter and Paul.
Who are they by my bed?
The lovely Bride and her Fosterling.
Who are those watching over my sleep?
The fair loving Mary and her Lamb.
Who is that anear me?
The King of the sun, He himself it is.
Who is that at the back of my head?
The Son of Life without beginning, without time.

84 Smooring the fire

The sacred Three
To save,
To shield,
To surround
The hearth,
The house,
The household,
This eve,
This night,
Oh! this eve,
This night,
And every night,
Each single night.
    Amen.

85 Smooring the fire

I will build the hearth,
As Mary would build it.
The encompassment of Bride and of Mary,
Guarding the hearth, guarding the floor,
Guarding the household all.

Who are they on the lawn without?
Michael the sun-radiant of my trust.
Who are they on the middle of the floor?
John and Peter and Paul.
Who are they by the front of my bed?
Sun-bright Mary and her Son.

The mouth of God ordained,
The angel of God proclaimed,
An angel white in charge of the hearth
Till white day shall come to the embers.
An angel white in charge of the hearth
Till white day shall come to the embers.

86 Blessing of the smooring

I am smooring the fire
As the Son of Mary would smoor;
Blest be the house, blest be the fire,
    Blest be the people all.

Who are those down on the floor?
John and Peter and Paul.
On whom is the vigil tonight?
    On the fair gentle Mary and on her Son.

The mouth of God said,
The angel of God spake,
An angel in the door of the house,

To guard and to keep us all
   Till comes daylight tomorrow.

Oh! may the angels of the Holy One of God
Environ me all this night,
Oh! may the angels of the Anointed One of God
Encompass me from harm and from evil,
   Oh! encompass me from harm this night.

87   Smooring blessing

I will smoor the hearth
As Mary would smoor;
The encompassment of Bride and of Mary,
On the fire and on the floor,
   And on the household all.

Who is on the lawn without?
Fairest Mary and her Son,
The mouth of God ordained, the angel of God spoke;
Angels of promise watching the hearth,
   Till white day comes to the fire.

88   The consecration of the seed

I will go out to sow the seed,
In name of Him who gave it growth;
I will place my front in the wind,
And throw a gracious handful on high.
Should a grain fall on a bare rock,
It shall have no soil in which to grow;
As much as falls into the earth,
The dew will make it to be full.

Friday, day auspicious,
The dew will come down to welcome
Every seed that lay in sleep
Since the coming of cold without mercy;
Every seed will take root in the earth,
As the King of the elements desired,
The braird will come forth with the dew,
It will inhale life from the soft wind.

I will come round with my step,
I will go rightways with the sun,
In name of Ariel and the angels nine,
In name of Gabriel and the Apostles kind.

Father, Son, and Spirit Holy,
Be giving growth and kindly substance
To every thing that is in my ground,
Till the day of gladness shall come.

The Feast day of Michael, day beneficent,
I will put my sickle round about
The root of my corn as was wont;
I will lift the first cut quickly;
I will put it three turns round
My head, saying my rune the while,
My back to the airt of the north;
My face to the fair sun of power.

I shall throw the handful far from me,
I shall close my two eyes twice,
Should it fall in one bunch
My stacks will be productive and lasting;
No Carlin will come with bad times
To ask a palm bannock from us,
What time rough storms come with frowns
Nor stint nor hardship shall be on us.

89   Reaping blessing

God, bless Thou Thyself my reaping,
Each ridge, and plain, and field,
Each sickle curved, shapely, hard,
Each ear and handful in the sheaf,
    Each ear and handful in the sheaf.

Bless each maiden and youth,
Each woman and tender youngling,
Safeguard them beneath Thy shield of strength,
And guard them in the house of the saints,
    Guard them in the house of the saints.

Encompass each goat, sheep and lamb,
Each cow and horse, and store,
Surround Thou the flocks and herds,
And tend them to a kindly fold,
    Tend them to a kindly fold.

For the sake of Michael head of hosts,
Of Mary fair-skinned branch of grace,
Of Bride smooth-white of ringleted locks,
Of Columba of the graves and tombs,
    Columba of the graves and tombs.

90   Reaping blessing

On Tuesday of the feast at the rise of the sun,
And the back of the ear of corn to the east,
I will go forth with my sickle under my arm,
And I will reap the cut the first act.

I will let my sickle down
While the fruitful ear is in my grasp,
I will raise mine eye upwards,
I will turn me on my heel quickly,

Rightway as travels the sun
From the airt of the east to the west,
From the airt of the north with motion calm
To the very core of the airt of the south.

I will give thanks to the King of grace
For the growing crops of the ground,
He will give food to ourselves and to the flocks
According as He disposeth to us.

James and John, Peter and Paul,
Mary beloved, the fullness of light,

  ★ ★ ★

On Michaelmas Eve and Christmas,
We will all taste of the bannock.

91   The blessing of the parching

Thou flame grey, slender, curved,
Coming from the top pore of the peat,
Thou flame of leaps, breadth, heat,
Come not nigh me with thy quips.

A burning steady, gentle, generous,
Coming round about my quicken roots,
A fire fragrant, fair, and peaceful,
Nor causes dust, nor grief, nor havoc.

Heat, parch my fat seed,
For food for my little child,
In name of Christ, King of the elements,
Who gave us corn and bread and blessing withal,
  In name of Christ, King of the elements,
   Who gave us corn and bread and blessing withal.

92   **The quern blessing**

On Ash Eve
We shall have flesh,
We should have that,
    We should have that.

The cheek of hen,
Two bits of barley,
That were enough,
    That were enough.

We shall have mead,
We shall have spruce,
We shall have wine,
We shall have feast.
We shall have sweetness and milk produce,
Honey and milk,
Wholesome ambrosia,
Abundance of that,
    Abundance of that.

We shall have harp,
We shall have pedal,
We shall have lute,
We shall have horn.
We shall have sweet psaltery
Of the melodious strings
And the regal lyre,
Of the songs we shall have,
    Of the songs we shall have.

The calm fair Bride will be with us,
The gentle Mary mother will be with us.
Michael the chief
Of glancing glaves,
And the King of kings
And Jesus Christ,
And the Spirit of peace

And of grace will be with us,
 Of grace will be with us.

93   Milking croon

Come, Brendan, from the ocean,
Come, Ternan, most potent of men,
Come, Michael valiant, down
And propitiate to me the cow of my joy.
 Ho my heifer, ho heifer of my love,
 Ho my heifer, ho heifer of my love.
 My beloved heifer, choice cow of every shieling,
 For the sake of the High King take to thy calf.

Come, beloved Colum of the fold,
Come, great Bride of the flocks,
Come, fair Mary from the cloud,
And propitiate to me the cow of my love.
 Ho my heifer, ho heifer of my love.

The stock-dove will come from the wood,
The tusk will come from the wave,
The fox will come but not with wiles,
To hail my cow of virtues.
 Ho my heifer, ho heifer of my love.

94   Milking croon

The charm placed of Mary of light,
Early and late going to and from home,
The herdsman Patrick and the milkmaid Bride,
Be saining you and saving you and shielding you.
 Ho hi holigan, ho my heifer,
 Ho hi holigan, ho my heifer,

Ho hi holigan, ho my heifer,
My calving kine on each side of the river.

A shackle of lint on my elfish heifer,
A shackle of silk on my heifer of calves,
A shackle of straw on the cows of the townland,
But a brand new shackle on my heifer beloved.
Ho hi holigan, ho my heifer.

Seest thou that cow on the plain
With her frisky calf before her?
Do, thou lovable one, as she did erstwhile,
Give thou thy milk, O calf of Fiannach.
Ho hi holigan, ho my heifer.

95   Milking blessing

Columba will give to her progeny,
Coivi the propitious, will give to her grass,
My speckled heifer will give me her milk,
And her female calf before her.
Ho my heifer! heifer! heifer!
Ho my heifer! kindly, calm,
My heifer gentle, gentle, beloved,
Thou art the love of thy mother.

Seest yonder thriving bramble bush
And the other bush glossy with brambles,
Such like is my fox-coloured heifer,
And her female calf before her.
Ho my heifer! heifer! heifer!

The calm Bride of the white combs
Will give to my loved heifer the lustre of the swan,
While the loving Mary, of the combs of honey,
Will give to her the mottle of the heather hen.
Ho my heifer! heifer! heifer!

96 Ho hoiligean, ho my heifers

My treasure thou, and thou art of the sea kine,
Red eared, notch eared, high horned;
Urine was sprinkled on the rump of thy grandsire,
And thou shalt not win from me on Monday nor Saturday.
>   Ho hoiligean, ho my heifers!
>   Ho hoiligean, ho my heifers!
>   Ho hoiligean, ho my heifers!
>   My kindly kine on each side of the stream.

My treasure thou, and thou art of the land kine,
Thou wilt give me milk produce, thou wilt give me dainty;
Thou wilt give me milk from the top of the club-moss,
And not the grey water of the sand-drift.
>   Ho hoiligean, ho my heifers!

My treasure thou, and thou art of the world's kine,
Thou wilt give me milk from the heather tops;
Not grey milk of the taste of the rowan berries,
But honey milk and white as the sea-gull.
>   Ho hoiligean, ho my heifers!

The melodious Bride will give thee offspring and young,
The lovely Mary will give thee colour to cover thee,
The lustrous Michael will give thee a star to guide thee,
And Christ Jesu will give thee peace and joy.
>   Ho hoiligean, ho my heifers!

97 Ho, my heifer!

The night the Herdsman was out
No shackle went on a cow,
Lowing ceased not from the mouth of calf
Wailing the Herdsman of the flock,
>   Wailing the Herdsman of the flock.

Ho my heifer! ho my heifer!
Ho my heifer! my heifer beloved!
My heartling heart, kind, fond,
For the sake of the High King take to thy calf.

The night the Herdsman was missing,
In the Temple He was found.
The King of the moon to come hither!
The King of the sun down from heaven!
　　King of the sun down from heaven!

98　Give thy milk

Give thy milk, brown cow,
For what reason should I conceal?
The skin of the calf of yonder cow on the partition,
While the calf of my love is on another grange.
　　Oh! ho! another grange.

　　Give thy milk, brown cow,
　　Give thy milk, brown cow,
　　Give thy milk, brown cow,
　　Heavily flowing.

My beloved shall get white-bellied calves,
And a fetter fine that shall go kindly round her legs;
No fetter of hair, nor of heather, nor of lint refuse,
But a dear fetter that men bring from Saxon land.
　　Oh! ho! from Saxon land.

And my queen maiden of beauty shall get
A fetter smooth to go softly round her legs;
No fetter of cord, nor of lint, nor lint refuse,
But a fetter of silk up from Saxon land.
　　Oh! ho! from Saxon land.

My beloved shall get grass and shelter,
She shall get hill, heath, and plain,

She shall get meadow-grass, club-rush, and stubble,
And she shall get the wine from the steep bens.
    Oh! ho! the steep bens.

99 Milking song

Come, Mary, and milk my cow,
Come, Bride, and encompass her,
Come, Columba the benign,
And twine thine arms around my cow.
    Ho my heifer, ho my gentle heifer,
    Ho my heifer, ho my gentle heifer,
    Ho my heifer, ho my gentle heifer,
    My heifer dear, generous and kind,
    For the sake of the High King take to thy calf.

Come, Mary Virgin, to my cow,
Come, great Bride, the beauteous,
Come, thou milkmaid of Jesus Christ,
And place thine arms beneath my cow.
    Ho my heifer, ho my gentle heifer.

Lovely black cow, pride of the shieling,
First cow of the byre, choice mother of calves,
Wisps of straw round the cows of the townland,
A shackle of silk on my heifer beloved.
    Ho my heifer, ho my gentle heifer.

My black cow, my black cow,
A like sorrow afflicts me and thee,
Thou grieving for thy lovely calf,
I for my beloved son under the sea,
    My beloved only son under the sea.

100   Herding blessing

The keeping of God and the Lord on you,
The keeping of Christ always on you,
The keeping of Carmac and of Columba on you,
The keeping of Cairbre on you going and coming,
And the keeping of Ariel the gold-bright on you,
    The king of Ariel the gold-bright on you.

The keeping of Bride the foster-mother on you,
The keeping of Mary the yellow-haired on you,
Of Christ Jesus, the Son of peace,
The King of kings, land and sea,
And the peace-giving Spirit, everlasting, be yours,
    The peace-giving Spirit, everlasting, be yours.

101   Herding blessing

I will place this flock before me,
As was ordained of the King of the world,
Bride to keep them, to watch them, to tend them,
On ben, on glen, on plain,
    Bride to keep them, to watch them, to tend them,
    On ben, on glen, on plain.

Arise, thou Bride the gentle, the fair,
Take thou thy lint, thy comb, and thy hair,
Since thou to them madest the noble charm,
To keep them from straying, to save them from harm,
    Since thou to them madest the noble charm,
    To keep them from straying, to save them from
        harm.

From rocks, from drifts, from streams,
From crooked passes, from destructive pits,
From the straight arrows of the slender ban-shee,
From the heart of envy, from the eye of evil,

From the straight arrows of the slender ban-shee,
From the heart of envy, from the eye of evil.

Mary Mother, tend thou the offspring, all,
Bride of the fair palms, guard thou my flocks,
Kindly Columba, thou saint of many powers,
Encompass thou the breeding cows, bestow on me herds,
　　Kindly Columba, thou saint of many powers,
　　　Encompass thou the breeding cows, bestow on me
　　　　herds.

102　Herding blessing

Travelling moorland, travelling townland,
Travelling mossland long and wide,
Be the herding of God the Son about your feet,
Safe and whole may ye home return,
　　Be the herding of God the Son about your feet,
　　Safe and whole may ye home return.

The sanctuary of Carmac and of Columba
Be protecting you going and coining,
And of the milkmaid of the soft palms,
Bride of the clustering hair golden brown,
　　And of the milkmaid of the soft palms,
　　Bride of the clustering hair golden brown.

103　The protection of the cattle

Pastures smooth, long, and spreading,
Grassy meads aneath your feet,
The friendship of God the Son to bring you home
To the field of the fountains,
　　Field of the fountains.

Closed be every pit to you,
Smoothed be every knoll to you,
Cosy every exposure to you.
Beside the cold mountains,
　　Beside the cold mountains.

The care of Peter and of Paul,
The care of James and of John,
The care of Bride fair and of Mary Virgin,
To meet you and to tend you,
　　Oh! the care of all the band
　　To protect you and to strengthen you.

104　Guarding the flocks

May Mary the mild keep the sheep,
May Bride the calm keep the sheep,
May Columba keep the sheep,
May Maolruba keep the sheep,
May Carmac keep the sheep,
From the fox and the wolf.

May Oran keep the kine,
May Modan keep the kine,
May Donnan keep the kine,
May Moluag keep the kine,
May Maolruan keep the kine,
On soft land and hard land.

May the Spirit of peace preserve the flocks,
May the Son of Mary Virgin preserve the flocks,
May the God of glory preserve the flocks,
May the Three preserve the flocks,
From wounding and from death-loss,
　　From wounding and from death-loss.

105   A herding croon

The cattle are today going a-flitting,
    Hill–i–ruin is o h–ug o,
    Ho ro la ill o,
    Hill–i–ruin is o h–ug o,
Going to eat the grass of the burial-place,
    Hill–i–ruin is o h–ug o,
Their own herdsman there to tend them,
      Ho ro la ill o,
    Hill–i–ruin is o h–ug o,
Tending them, fending them, turning them,
    Hill–i–ruin is o h–ug o,
Be the gentle Bride milking them,
    Hill–i–ruin is o h–ug o,
Be the lovely Mary keeping them,
    Hill i–ruin is o h–ug o,
And Jesu Christ at the end of their journey,
Jesu Christ at the end of their journey.
    Hill–i–ruin is o h–ug o.

106   Hatching blessing

I will rise early on the morning of Monday.
I will sing my rune and rhyme,
I will go sunwise with my cog
To the nest of my hen with sure intent.

I will place my left hand to my breast,
My right hand to my heart,
I will seek the loving wisdom of Him
Abundant in grace, in broods, and in flocks.

I will close my two eyes quickly,
As in blind-man's buff moving, slowly;
I will stretch my left hand over thither
To the nest of my hen on yonder side.

The first egg which I shall bring near me,
I will put it withershins round my head.
[I will life the egg down in my right hand,
There shall then be one in the cog.]

I will raise my left hand on high,
I will stretch it without halt quickly,
I will lift the two eggs down hither,
There shall be then three in the cog.

I will stretch my right hand again,
I will lift with it at the time three,
I will seek ruling from the King,
Then verily there shall be six in the clutch.

I will raise my left hand the second time,
I will lift four with it down,
In name of Christ, King of power,
There shall then be ten in the cog.

The right fist of strongest claim,
I will lift with it two in my fingers,
Thus at ceasing my brood will be complete,
Beneath the breast of the speckled big hen.

I will put soot on their two ends,
And I dumb as the dumb the while,
In name of Creator of sea and hill,
In name of saints and apostles all.

In name of the most Holy Trinity,
In name of Columba kindly,
I will set the eggs on Thursday,
The gladsome brood will come on Friday.

107 Marking the lambs

My knife will be new, keen, clean, without stain,
My plaid beneath my knee with my red robe,
I will put sunwise round my breast the first cut for luck,
The next one after that with the sun as it moves.

A male lamb without blemish, of one colour, without
    defect,
Allow thou out on the plain, nor his flowing blood
    check,
If the froth remains on the heather with red top,
My flock will be without flaw as long as I change not
    the name.

The Three who are above in the City of glory,
Be shepherding my flock and my kine,
Tending them duly in heat, in storm, and in cold,
With the blessing of power driving them down
From yonder height to the sheiling fold.

The name of Ariel of beauteous bloom,
The name of Gabriel herald of the Lamb,
The name of Raphael prince of power,
Surrounding them and saving them.

The name of Muriel and of Mary Virgin,
The name of Peter and of Paul,
The name of James and of John,
Each angel and apostle on their track,
Keeping them alive and their progeny,
        Keeping them alive and their progeny.

108   The clipping blessing

Go shorn and come woolly,
Bear the Beltane female lamb,
Be the lovely Bride thee endowing,
And the fair Mary thee sustaining,
      The fair Mary sustaining thee.

Michael the chief be shielding thee
From the evil dog and from the fox,
From the wolf and from the sly bear,
And from the taloned birds of destructive bills,
      From the taloned birds of hooked bills.

109   The chant of the warping

Thursday of beneficence,
For warping and waulking,
A hundred and fifty strands there shall be
      To number.

Blue thread, very fine,
Two of white by its side,
And scarlet by the side
      Of the madder.

My warp shall be very even,
Give to me Thy blessing, O God,
And to all who are beneath my roof
      In the dwelling.

Michael, thou angel of power,
Mary fair, who art above,
Christ, Thou Shepherd of the people,
Do ye your eternal blessing
      Bestow

On each one who shall lie down,
In name of the Father and of Christ,
And of the Spirit of peacefulness,
　　And of grace.

Sprinkle down on us like dew
The gracious wisdom of the mild woman,
Who neglected never the guidance
　　Of the High King.

Ward away every evil eye,
And all people of evil wishes,
Consecrate the woof and the warp
　　Of every thread.

Place Thou Thine arm around
Each woman who shall be waulking it,
And do Thou aid her in the hour
　　Of her need.

Give to me virtues abundant,
As Mary had in her day,
That I may possess the glory
　　Of the High King

Since Thou, O God, it is who givest growth,
To each species and kind,
Give us wool from the surface
　　Of the green grass.

Consecrate the flock in every place,
With their little lambs melodious, innocent,
And increase the generations
　　Of our herds.

So that we may obtain from them wool,
And nourishing milk to drink,
And that no dearth may be ours
　　Of day clothing.

110   Loom blessing

Thrums nor odds of thread
My hand never kept, nor shall keep,

Every colour in the bow of the shower
Has gone through my fingers beneath the cross,

White and black, red and madder,
Green, dark grey, and scarlet,

Blue, and roan and colour of the sheep,
And never a particle of cloth was wanting.
I beseech calm Bride the generous,
I beseech mild Mary the loving,
I beseech Christ Jesu the humane,
That I may not die without them,
    That I may not die without them.

111   Setting the *iomairt*

The black by the white,
The white by the black,
The green in the middle of the red,
The red in the middle of the black.

The black in the middle of the red,
The red in the middle of the white,
The white in the middle of the green,
The green in the middle of the white.

The white in the middle of the blue,
The blue in the middle of the scarlet;
  . . .
  . . .
The scarlet to the blue,
The blue to the scarlet,

The scarlet to the black,
The black to the scarlet.

A thread to two threads
Of two colours,
Two threads of black
To one thread of white.

Seven threads to five,
Five to three,
Three to two,
Two to one,
In each border.

112   Loom blessing

Bless, O Chief of generous chiefs,
My loom and everything anear me,
Bless me in my every action,
Make Thou me safe while I live.

From every brownie and fairy woman,
From every evil wish and sorrow,
Help me, O Thou helping Being,
As long as I shall be in the land of the living.

In name of Mary, mild of deeds,
In name of Columba, just and potent,
Consecrate the four posts of my loom,
Till I begin on Monday.

Her pedals, her sleay, and her shuttle,
Her reeds, her warp, and her cogs,
Her cloth-beam, and her thread-beam,
Thrums and the thread of the plies.

Every web, black, white, and fair,
Roan, dun, checked, and red,

Give Thy blessing everywhere,
On every shuttle passing under the thread.

Thus will my loom be unharmed,
Till I shall arise on Monday;
Beauteous Mary will give me of her hove,
And there shall be no obstruction I shall not overcome.

113   The consecration of the cloth

Well can I say my rune,
Descending with the glen;
>One rune,
>Two runes,
>Three runes,
>Four runes,
>Five runes,
>Six runes.
>Seven runes,
>Seven and a half runes,
>Seven and a half runes.

May the man of this clothing never be wounded,
May torn he never be;
What time he goes into battle or combat,
May the sanctuary shield of the Lord be his.
>What time he goes into battle or combat,
>May the sanctuary shield of the Lord be his.

This is not second clothing and it is not thigged,
Nor is it the right of sacristan or of priest.

Cresses green culled beneath a stone,
And given to a woman in secret.
The shank of the deer in the head of the herring,
And in the slender tail of the speckled salmon.

114   Hunting blessing

From my loins begotten wert thou, my son,
May I guide thee the way that is right,
In the holy name of the apostles eleven
In name of the Son of God torn of thee.

In name of James, and Peter, and Paul,
John the baptist, and John the apostle above,
Luke the physician, and Stephen the martyr,
Muriel the fair, and Mary mother of the Lamb.

In name of Patrick holy of the deeds,
And Carmac of the rights and tombs,
Columba beloved, and Adamnan of laws,
Fite calm, and Bride of the milk and kine.

In name of Michael chief of hosts,
In name of Ariel youth of lovely hues,
In name of Uriel of the golden locks,
And Gabriel seer of the Virgin of grace.

The time thou shalt have closed thine eye,
Thou shalt not bend thy knee nor move,
Thou shalt not wound the duck that is swimming,
Never shalt thou harry her of her young.

The white swan of the sweet gurgle,
The speckled dun of the brown tuft,
Thou shalt not cut a feather from their backs,
Till the doom-day, on the crest of the wave.

On the wing be they always
Ere thou place missile to thine ear,
And the fair Mary will give thee of her love,
And the lovely Bride will give thee of her kine.

Thou shalt not eat fallen fish nor fallen flesh,
Nor one bird that thy hand shall not bring down,
Be thou thankful for the one,
Though nine should be swimming.

The fairy swan of Bride of flocks,
The fairy duck of Mary of peace.

115   Consecrating the chase

In name of the Holy Threefold as one,
In word, in deed, and in thought,
I am bathing mine own hands,
In the light and in the elements of the sky.

Vowing that I shall never return in my life,
Without fishing, without fowling either,
Without game, without venison down from the hill,
Without fat, without blubber from out the copse.

O Mary tender-fair, gentle-fair, loving-fair,
Avoid thou to me the silvery salmon dead on the salt sea,
A duck with her brood and it please thee to show me,
A nest by the edge of the water where it does not dry.

The grey-hen on the crown of the knoll,
The black-cock of the hoarse croon,
After the strength of the sun has gone down,
Avoid, oh, avoid thou to me the hearing of them.

O Mary, fragrant mother of my King,
Crown thou me with the crown of thy peace,
Place thine own regal robe of gold to protect me,
And save me with the saving of Christ,
Save me with the saving of Christ.

116   Prayer for travelling

Life be in my speech,
Sense in what I say,
The bloom of cherries on my lips,
Till I come back again.

The love Christ Jesus gave
Be filling every heart for me,
The love Christ Jesus gave
Filling me for every one.

Traversing corries, traversing forests,
Traversing valleys long and wild.
The fair white Mary still uphold me,
The Shepherd Jesu be my shield,
  The fair white Mary still uphold me,
  The Shepherd Jesu be my shield.

117   Fishing blessing

The day of light has come upon us,
Christ is born of the Virgin.

In His name I sprinkle the water
Upon every thing within my court.

Thou King of deeds and powers above,
Thy fishing blessing pour down on us.

I will sit me down with an oar in my grasp,
I will row me seven hundred and seven strokes.

I will cast down my hook,
The first fish which I bring up

In the name of Christ, King of the elements,
The poor shall have it at his wish.

And the king of fishers, the brave Peter,
He will after it give me his blessing.

Ariel, Gabriel, and John,
Raphael benign, and Paul,

Columba, tender in every distress,
And Mary fair, the endowed of grace.

Encompass ye us to the fishing-bank of ocean,
And still ye to us the crest of the waves.

Be the King of kings at the end of our course,
Of lengthened life and of lasting happiness.

Be the crown of the King from the Three on high,
Be the cross of Christ adown to shield us,
  The crown of the King from the Three above,
  The cross of Christ adown to shield us.

118 The ocean blessing

O Thou who pervadest the heights,
Imprint on us Thy gracious blessing,
Carry us over the surface of the sea,
Carry us safely to a haven of peace,
Bless our boatmen and our boat,
Bless our anchors and our oars,
Each stay and halyard and traveller,
Our mainsails to our tall masts
Keep, O King of the elements, in their place
That we may return home in peace;
I myself will sit down at the helm,
It is God's own Son who will give me guidance,
As He gave to Columba the mild
What time he set stay to sails.

Mary, Bride, Michael, Paul,
Peter, Gabriel, John of love,
Pour ye down from above the dew
That would make our faith to grow,
Establish ye us in the Rock of rocks,
In every law that love exhibits,
That we may reach the land of glory,
Where peace and love and mercy reign,
All vouchsafed to us through grace;
Never shall the canker worm get near us,
We shall there be safe for ever,
We shall not be in the bonds of death
Though we are of the seed of Adam.

On the Feast Day of Michael, the Feast Day of Martin,
The Feast Day of Andrew, band of mercy,
The Feast Day of Bride, day of my choice,
Cast ye the serpent into the ocean,
So that the sea may swallow her up;
On the Feast Day of Patrick, day of power,
Reveal to us the storm from the north,
Quell its wrath and blunt its fury,
Lessen its fierceness, kill its cold.

On the Day of the Three Kings on high,
Subdue to us the crest of the waves,
On Beltane Day give us the dew,
On John's Day the gentle wind,
The Day of Mary the great of fame,
Ward off us the storm from the west;
Each day and night, storm and calm,
Be Thou with us, O Chief of chiefs,
Be Thou Thyself to us a compass-chart,
Be Thine hand on the helm of our rudder,
Thine own hand, Thou God of the elements,
Early and late as is becoming,
    Early and late as is becoming.

119   Ocean blessing

God the Father all-powerful, benign,
Jesu the Son of tears and of sorrow,
With thy co-assistance, O Holy Spirit!

The Three-One, ever-living, ever-mighty, everlasting,
Who brought the Children of Israel through
    the Red Sea,
And Jonah to land from the belly of the great creature
    of the ocean,

Who brought Paul and his companions in the ship,
From the torment of the sea, from the dolour
    of the waves,
From the gale that was great, from the storm that
    was heavy.

Sain us and shield and sanctify us,
Be Thou, King of the elements, seated at our helm,
And lead us in peace to the end of our journey.

With winds mild, kindly, benign, pleasant.
Without swirl, without whirl, without eddy,
That would do no harmful deed to us.

We ask all things of Thee, O God,
According to Thine own will and word.

120   Ruler of the elements

The Children of Israel, God taking them,
    Through the Red Sea obtained a path,
They obtained the quenching of their thirst
    From a rock that might not by craftsman be hewn.

Who are they on the tiller of my rudder,
    Giving speed to my east bound barge?

Peter and Paul and John the beloved,
    Three to whom laud and obeisance are due.

Who are the group near to my helm?
    Peter and Paul and John the Baptist;
Christ is sitting on my helm,
    Making guidance to the wind from the south.

To whom does tremble the voice of the wind?
    To whom become tranquil strait and ocean?
To Jesus Christ, Chief of each saint,
    Son of Mary, Root of victory,
    Son of Mary, Root of victory.

121   Sea prayer

HELMSMAN: Blest be the boat.

CREW: God the Father bless her.

HELMSMAN: Blest be the boat.

CREW: God the Son bless her.

HELMSMAN: Blest be the boat.

CREW: God the Spirit bless her.

ALL: God the Father,
              God the Son,
              God the Spirit,
              Bless the boat.

HELMSMAN: What can befall you
              And God the Father with you?

CREW: No harm can befall us.

HELMSMAN: What can befall you
              And God the Son with you?

CREW: No harm can befall us.

HELMSMAN: What can befall you
             And God the Spirit with you?

CREW: No harm can befall us.

ALL: God the Father,
             God the Son,
             God the Spirit,
             With us eternally.

HELMSMAN: What can cause you anxiety
             And the God of the elements over you?

CREW: No anxiety can be ours.

HELMSMAN: What can cause you anxiety
             And the King of the elements over you?

CREW: No anxiety can be ours.

HELMSMAN: What can cause you anxiety
             And the Spirit of the elements over you?

CREW: No anxiety can be ours.

ALL: The God of the elements,
             The King of the elements,
             The Spirit of the elements,
             Close over us,
             Ever eternally.

Incantations

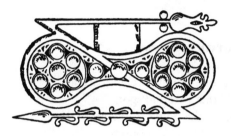

122 Charm for rose

Behold, Son and Christ,
The breast of Thy Mother swollen;
Give Thou peace to the breast,
Subdue Thou the swelling;
> Give Thou peace to the breast,
> Subdue Thou the swelling.

Behold it thyself, Queen,
Since of thee the Son was born,
Appease thou the breast,
Subdue thou the swelling;
> Appease thou the breast,
> Subdue thou the swelling.

See Thou it, Jesu,
Since Thou art King of life;
Appease Thou the breast,
Subdue Thou the udder;
> Appease Thou the breast,
> Subdue Thou the udder.

I behold, said Christ,
And I do as is meet,
I give ease to the breast,
And rest to the udder;
I give ease to the breast,
And rest to the udder.

123   Charm for rose

Thou rose windy, swelling, deadly,
Leave that part and spot,
There is the udder in the ground,
And leave the breast.

See, Christ, the woman
And her breast swollen,
See her thyself, Mary,
It was thou didst bear the Son.

Thou rose windy, deadly, thirsty,
Leave the breast and the spot,
And take thyself off;
Healed be the breast,
Withered be the swelling.

Flee thieving red one,
Flee quickly thieving one,
Swelling that was in the breast,
Leave the udder and the breast,
And flee hence.

124   Charm for rose

Thou rose deathly, deadly, swollen,
Leave the udder of the white-footed cow,
Leave the udder of the spotted cow,
Leave, leave that swelling,
And betake thyself to other swelling.

Thou rose thrawn, obstinate,
Surly in the udder of the cow,
Leave thou the swelling and the udder,
Flee to the bottom of the stone.

I place the rose to the stone,
I place the stone to the earth,
I place milk in the udder,
I place substance in the kidney.

125   Charm for swollen breast

The charm made by Gillecaluim,
On the one cow of the carlin,
For rose, for hardness, for pain,
For swelling, for lump, for growth,
For uzzening, for udder, for milking,
For the three *corracha crith,*
For the three *corracha cnamh,*
For the three *corracha creothail,*
Do not deny it to beast,
Do not refuse it to wife,
Do not withhold it on Sunday.
The charm made of generous Fionn,
To his very sister,
For rose, for hardness,
For swelling of breast.

126   Toothache charm

The incantation put by lovely Bride
Before the thumb of the Mother of God,
On lint, on wort, on hemp,
For worm, for venom, for teeth.

The worm that tortured me,
In the teeth of my head,
Hell hard by my teeth,
The teeth of hell distressing me.

The teeth of hell close to me;
As long as I myself shall last
May my teeth last in my head.

127   Charm for jaundice

For the jaundice, for the spaul, for the bloody flux,
For the red disease, for the withering disease,
For the bot disease, for the skin disease,
For the brown disease, for the foot disease,
And for every disease that might be
In the constitution of cow
Or adhering to stirk.

128   Charm for a bursting vein

The rune made by the holy maiden Bride
To the lame mariner,
For knee, for crookedness, for crippleness,
For the nine painful diseases, for the three venomous
    diseases,
Refuse it not to beast, deny it not to dame.

Christ went on a horse,
A horse broke his leg,
Christ went down,
He made whole the leg.

As Christ made whole that,
May Christ make whole this,
And more than this,
If it be His will so to do.

The charm made by Columba,
On the bottom of the glen,
For bursting of vein, for dislocation of bone:
Thou art ill today, thou shalt be well tomorrow.

129   Charm for bursting vein

Rosary of Mary, one,
Rosary of Mary, two,
Rosary of Mary, three,
Rosary of Mary, four,
Rosary of Mary, five,
Rosary of Mary, six,
Rosary of Mary, seven,
Seven Rosaries of Mary ever
Between pain and ease,
Between sole and summit,
Between health and grave.

Christ went on an ass,
She sprained her foot,
He came down
And healed her foot;
As He healed that
May He heal this,
And greater than this,
If it be His will to do.

130   Charm of the sprain

Bride went out
In the morning early,
With a pair of horses;
One broke his leg,
With much ado,
That was apart,
She put bone to bone,
She put flesh to flesh,
She put sinew to sinew,
She put vein to vein;
As she healed that
May I heal this.

131   Charm for sprain

Christ went on the cross,
Sprained the leg of a horse;
Christ came to the ground,
Whole became the leg.

As that was made whole
May this become whole,
If His will be so to do,
Through the bosom of the God of life,
And of the Three of the Trinity,
    The God of life,
    The Three of Trinity.

132   Charm for sprain

Christ went out
In the morning early,
He found the legs of the horses
In fragments soft;
He put marrow to marrow,
He put pith to pith,
He put bone to bone,
He put membrane to membrane,
He put tendon to tendon,
He put blood to blood,
He put tallow to tallow,
He put flesh to flesh,
He put fat to fat,
He put skin to skin,
He put hair to hair,
He put warm to warm,
He put cool to cool,
As the King of power healed that
It is in His nature to heal this,
If it be His own will to do it.
    Through the bosom of the Being of life,
    And of the Three of the Trinity.

133   Fath-fith

Fath-fith
Will I make on thee,
By Mary of the augury,
By Bride of the corslet,
From sheep, from ram,
From goat, from buck,
From fox, from wolf,
From sow, from boar,

From dog, from cat,
From hipped-bear,
From wilderness-dog,
From watchful *scan*, ★
From cow, from horse,
From bull, from heifer,
From daughter, from son,
From the birds of the air,
From the creeping things of the earth,
From the fishes of the sea,
From the imps of the storm.

134   Charm of the lasting life

I place the charm on thy body,
And on thy prosperity,
The charm of the God of life
For thy protection.

The charm that Bride of the kine
Put round the fair neck of Dornghil,
The charm that Mary put about her Son,
Between sole and throat,
Between pap and knee,
Between back and breast,
Between chest and sole,
Between eye and hair.

The host of Michael on thy side,
The shield of Michael on thy shoulder,
There is not between heaven and earth
That can overcome the King of grace.

No spear shall rive thee,
No sea shall drown thee,

★Probably some animal.

No woman shall wile thee,
No man shall wound thee.

The mantle of Christ Himself about thee,
The shadow of Christ Himself above thee,
From the crown of thy head
To the soles of thy feet.
The charm of God is on thee now,
Thou shalt never know disgrace.

Thou shalt go forth in name of thy King,
Thou shalt come in in name of thy Chief,
To the God of life thou now belongest wholly,
And to all the Powers together.

I place this charm early on Monday,
In passage hard, brambly, thorny,
Go thou out and the charm about thy body,
And be not the least fear upon thee.

Thou shalt ascend the crest of the hill,
Protected thou shalt be behind thee,
Thou art the calm swan in battle,
Preserved thou shalt be amidst the slaughter,
Stand thou canst against five hundred,
And thine oppressors shall be seized.

The charm of God about thee!
The arm of God above thee!

135   The charm of the lasting life

I will place the charm of the lasting life,
Upon your cattle active, broad, and full,
The knoll upon which the herds shall lie down,
That they may rise from it whole and well.

Down with success, and with blessing,
Up with activity and following,
Without envy, without malice, without ill-will,
Without small eye, without large eye,
Without the five eyes of neglect.

I will suck this, the sucking of envious vein
On the head of the house, and the townland families,
That every evil trait, and every evil tendency
Inherent in you shall cleave to them.

> If tongue cursed you,
> A heart blessed you;
> If eye blighted you,
> A wish prospered you.

A hurly-burlying, a topsy-turvying,
A hard hollying and a wan withering
To their female sheep and to their male calves,
For the nine and the nine score years.

136   St. Bride's charm

The charm put by Bride the beneficent,
On her goats, on her sheep, on her kine,
On her horses, on her chargers, on her herds,
Early and late going home, and from home.

To keep them from rocks and ridges,
From the heels and the horns of one another,
From the birds of the Red Rock,
And from Luath of the Feinne.

From the blue peregrine hawk of Creag Duilion,
From the brindled eagle of Ben-Ard,
From the swift hawk of Tordun,
From the surly raven of Bard's Creag.

From the fox of the wiles,
From the wolf of the Mam,
From the foul-smelling fumart,
And from the restless great-hipped bear.

From . . .
From . . .
From every hoofed of four feet,
And from every hatched of two wings.

137   Sain

The sain put by Mary on her Son,
Sain from death, sain from wound,
Sain from breast to knee,
Sain from knee to foot,
Sain of the three sains,
Sain of the five sains,
Sain of the seven sains,
From the crown of thy head
To the soles of thy feet.
Sain of the seven paters, one,
Sain of the seven paters, two,
Sain of the seven paters, three,
Sain of the seven paters, four,
Sain of the seven paters, five,
Sain of the seven paters, six,
Sain of the seven paters, seven
        Upon thee now.
From the edge of thy brow,
To thy coloured soles,
To preserve thee from behind,
To sustain thee in front.

Be the helmet of salvation about thine head,
Be the corslet of the covenant about thy throat,

Be the breastplate of the priest upon thy breast,
To shield thee in the battle and combat of thine enemies.

If pursued, oh youth, from behind thy back,
The power of the Virgin be close to succour thee,
East or west, west or east,
North or south, south or north.

138 Love charm

It is not love knowledge to thee
To draw water through a reed,
But the love of him [her] thou choosest,
With his [her] warmth to draw to thee.

Arise thou early on the day of the Lord,
To the broad flat flag,
Take with thee the foxglove
And the butterbur.

Lift them on thy shoulder
In a wooden shovel,
Get thee nine stems of ferns
Cut with an axe,

The three bones of an old man,
That have been drawn from the grave,
Burn them on a fire of faggots,
And make them all into ashes.

Shake it in the very breast of thy lover,
Against the sting of the north wind,
And I will pledge, and warrant thee,
That man [woman] will never leave thee.

139 Love charm

A love charm for thee,
Water drawn through a straw,
The warmth of him [her] thou lovest,
    With love to draw on thee.

Arise betimes on Lord's day,
To the flat rock of the shore
Take with thee the butterbur
    And the foxglove.

A small quantity of embers
In the skirt of thy kirtle,
A special handful of sea-weed
    In a wooden shovel.

Three bones of an old man,
Newly torn from the grave,
Nine stalks of royal fern,
    Newly trimmed with an axe.

Burn them on a fire of faggots
And make them all into ashes;
Sprinkle in the fleshy breast of thy lover,
    Against the venom of the north wind.

Go round the *rath* of procreation,
The circuit of the five turns,
And I will vow and warrant thee
    That man [woman] shall never leave thee.

140 Thwarting the evil eye

Who shall thwart the evil eye?
I shall thwart it, methinks,
In name of the King of life.
Three seven commands so potent,

Spake Christ in the door of the city;
    Pater Mary one,
    Pater King two,
    Pater Mary three,
    Pater King four,
    Pater Mary five,
    Pater King six,
    Pater Mary seven;
Seven pater Maries will thwart
    The evil eye,
Whether it be on man or on beast,
    On horse or on cow;
Be thou in thy full health this night,
    [*The name*]
In name of the Father, the Son, and the Holy Spirit.
    Amen.

141   Exorcism of the eye

I trample upon the eye,
As tramples the duck upon the lake,
As tramples the swan upon the water,
As tramples the horse upon the plain,
As tramples the cow upon the *iuc,*
As tramples the host of the elements,
    As tramples the host of the elements.

Power of wind I have over it,
Power of wrath I have over it,
Power of fire I have over it,
Power of thunder I have over it,
Power of lightning I have over it,
Power of storms I have over it,
Power of moon I have over it,
Power of sun I have over it,
Power of stars I have over it,

Power of firmament I have over it,
Power of the heavens
And of the worlds I have over it,
 Power of the heavens
  And of the worlds I have over it.

A portion of it upon the grey stones,
A portion of it upon the steep hills,
A portion of it upon the fast falls,
A portion of it upon the fair meads,
And a portion upon the great salt sea,
She herself is the best instrument to carry it,
 The great salt sea,
  The best instrument to carry it.

In name of the Three of Life,
In name of the Sacred Three,
In name of all the Secret Ones,
And of the Powers together.

142 Counteracting the evil eye

An eye covered thee,
A mouth spoke thee,
A heart envied thee,
A mind desired thee.

Four made thee thy cross,
Man and wife,
Youth and maid;
Three will I send to thwart them,
 Father,
 Son,
 Spirit Holy.

I appeal to Mary,
Aidful mother of men,

I appeal to Bride,
Foster-mother of Christ omnipotent,
I appeal to Columba,
Apostle of shore and sea,
And I appeal to heaven,
To all saints and angels that be above.

If it be a man that has done thee harm,
With evil eye,
With evil wish,
With evil passion,
Mayest thou cast off each ill,
Every malignity,
Every malice,
Every harassment,
And mayest thou be well for ever,
While this thread
Goes round thee,
In honour of God and of Jesus,
And of the Spirit of balm everlasting.

143   Spell for evil eye

The fair spell that lovely Mary sent,
Over stream, over sea, over land,
Against incantations, against withering glance,
Against inimical power,
Against the teeth of wolf,
Against the testicles of wolf,
Against the three crooked cranes,
Against the three crooked bones,
Against the three crooked *creothail*,
And against the long lint of the ground.

Whoso made to thee the eye,
May it lie upon himself,

May it lie upon his house,
May it lie upon his flocks,
May it lie upon his substance,
May it lie upon his fatness,
May it lie upon his means,
May it lie upon his children,
May it lie upon his wife,
May it lie upon his descendants.

I will subdue the eye,
I will suppress the eye,
And I will banish the eye,
The three arteries inviting
And the tongue of death completely.
Three lovely little maidens,
Born the same night with Christ,
If alive be these three tonight,
Life be anear thee, poor beast.

144 Charm for the eye

I place this charm to mine eye,
As the King of life ordained,
From the bosom of Peter and Paul,
The third best amulet under the sun.

Pour Mary, pour Bride,
Pour Patrick, king of laws,
Pour Columba the kindly,
Pour Ciaran, saint of power.

For victory in battle, for hardness of hand,
In battle of defence, in battle of offence,
On every son with whom it shall go well,
The Son of God will be with him in full armour.

From the bosom of Father,
From the bosom of Son,

From the bosom of Holy Spirit.
Amen.

145   Charm for the evil eye

Whoso laid on thee the eye,
May it lie upon himself.
May it lie upon his house,
May it lie upon his flocks,
On the shuffling carlin,
On the sour-faced carlin,
On the bounding carlin,
On the sharp-shanked carlin,
Who arose in the morning,
With her eye on her flocks,
With her flocks in her *seoin*,★
May she never own a fold,
May she never have half her desires,
The part of her which the ravens do not eat,
May the birds devour.

Four made to thee the eye,
Man and dame, youth and maid;
Three who will cast off thee the envy,
The Father, the Son, and the Holy Spirit.

As Christ lifted the fruit,
From the branches of the bushes,
May He now lift off thee
Every ailment, every envy, every jealousy,
From this day forth till the last day of thy life.

★Thoughts or mind.

146   Charm

Peter and James and John,
The three of sweetest virtues in glory,
Who arose to make the charm,
Before the great door of the City,
By the right knee of God the Son.

Against the keen-eyed men,
Against the peering-eyed women,
Against the slim, slender, fairy-darts,
Against the swift arrows of furies.

Two made to thee the withered eye,
Man and woman with venom and envy,
Three whom I will set against them,
Father, Son, and Spirit Holy.

Four and twenty diseases in the constitution of man and beast,
God scrape them, God search them, God cleanse them,
From out thy blood, from out thy flesh, from out thy fragrant
bones,
From this day and each day that comes, till thy day on earth
be done.

147   A malediction

There came two out
From the City of Heaven,
A man and a woman,
To make the *oisnean*.

Curses on the blear-eyed women,
Curses on the sharp-eyed men,
Curses on the four venomous arrows of disease,
That may be in the constitution of man and beast.

148   Spell of the evil eye

Trample I upon the eye,
As tramples the swan on a bare strand,
Power of wind I have over it,
The power of the Son of the King of Heaven
And of earth I have over it,
A portion of it on the grey stones,
*   *   *
And a portion on the great sea,
She herself is the instrument most able to bear it.

149   Incantation for the eye

Incantation of the seeing eye,
Incantation of the guiding star,
Incantation of the King of all kings,
Incantation of the God of life,
Incantation of the King of all kings,
Incantation of the God of life.

Incantation of Bride of the locks of gold,
Incantation of the beauteous Mary Virgin,
Incantation of the Virtue of all virtues,
Incantation of the God of glory,
Incantation of the Virtue of all virtues,
Incantation of the God of glory.

Incantation of Peter and of Paul,
Incantation of Ariel and John of love,
Incantation of the God of all gods,
Incantation of the God of grace,
Incantation of the God of all gods,
Incantation of the God of grace.

Feast of Mary, Feast of God,
Feast of cleric and of priest,

Feast of Christ, Prince of power,
Who established the sun with strength,
Feast of Christ, Prince of power,
Who endowed the sun with strength.

150   Spell of the eye

I place this spell to mine eye,
As the King of life ordained,
Spell of Peter, spell of Paul,
Spell of James, spell of John,
Spell of Columba benign,
Spell of Patrick, chief of saints,
Spell of Bride, tranquil of the kine,
Spell of Mary, lovely of the joys,
Spell of cows, spell of herds,
Spell of sheep, spell of flocks,
Spell of greatness, spell of means,
Spell of joy, spell of peace,
Spell of war, spell of the brave,
The third best spell under the sun,
The powerful spell of the Three Powers,
Father, Son, Spirit everlasting.

151   Spell of the eye

The spell fair-white,
Sent of Mary Virgin,
To the daughter of Dorail,
Of the golden-yellow hair,
Hither on mainland,
Hither on coastland,
Hither on lakeland,
Hither on ocean,

To thwart eye,
To thwart net,
To thwart envy,
To thwart hate.
To repel *breotaich,*
To repel *greotaich,*
To repel *sreotaich,*
To repel rose.

152   Spell of the eye

The spell the great white Mary sent
To Bride the lovely fair,
For sea, for land, for water, and for withering glance,
For teeth of wolf, for testicle of wolf.

Whoso laid on thee the eye,
May it oppress himself,
May it oppress his house,
May it oppress his flocks.

Let me subdue the eye,
Let me avert the eye,
The three complete tongues of fullness,
In the arteries of the heart,
In the vitals of the navel.

> From the bosom of Father,
> From the bosom of Son,
> From the bosom of Holy Spirit.

153   Spell of the counteracting

I will pluck the gracious yarrow
That Christ plucked with His one hand.

The High King of the angels
Came with His love and His countenance above me.

Jesus Christ came hitherward
With milk, with substance, with produce,
With female calves, with milk product.

On small eye, on large eye,
Over Christ's property.

In name of the Being of life
Supply me with Thy grace,
The crown of the King of the angels
To put milk in udder and gland,
With female calves, with progeny.

May you have the length of seven years
Without loss of calf, without loss of milk,
Without loss of means or of dear friends.

154   The counting of the stye

Why came the one stye,
Without the two styes here?
Why came the two styes,
Without the three styes here?
Why came the three styes,
Without the four styes here?
Why came the four styes,
Without the five styes here?
Why came the five styes,
Without the six styes here?
Why came the six styes,

Without the seven styes here?
Why came the seven styes,
Without the eight styes here?
Why came the eight styes,
Without the nine styes here?
Why came the nine,
Or one at all here?

155   The *fionn-faoilidh*

I place the *fionn-faoilidh*★ on me,
To drain wrath empty,
To preserve to me my fame,
While I shall live on earth.

O Michael! grasp my hand,
Vouchsafe to me the love of God,
If there be ill-will or ill-wish in mine enemy,
Christ be between me and him,
    Oh, Christ between me and him!

If there be ill-will or ill-wish concerning me,
Christ be between me and it,
    Oh, Christ between me and it!

156   Envy spell

Whoso made to thee the envy,
Swarthy man or woman fair,
Three I will send to thwart it:
Holy Spirit, Father, Son.

★A plant, the English name of which I do not know.

157 The red stalk

Pluck will I the little red-stalk of surety,
The lint the lovely Bride drew through her palm,
For success of health, for success of friendship,
    For success of joyousness,
For overcoming of evil mind, for overcoming of evil eye,
    For overcoming of bewitchment,
For overcoming of evil deed, for overcoming of evil
    conduct,
    For overcoming of malediction,
For overcoming of evil news, for overcoming of evil
    words,
    For success of blissfulness,
    For success of blissfulness.

158 The tree-entwining ivy

I will pluck the tree-entwining ivy,
As Mary plucked with her one hand,
As the King of life has ordained,
To put milk in udder and gland,
With speckled fair female calves,
As was spoken in the prophecy,
On this foundation for a year and a day,
Through the bosom of the God of life, and of all the
    powers.

159 The charm of the figwort

I will pluck the figwort,
With the fruitage of sea and land,
The plant of joy and gladness,
The plant of rich milk.

As the King of kings ordained,
To put milk in pap and gland,
As the Being of life ordained,
To place substance in udder and kidney,
With milk, with milkiness, with buttermilk,
With produce, with whisked whey, with milk-product,
With speckled female calves,
Without male calves,
With progeny, with joy, with fruitage,
With love, with charity, with bounty;

Without man of evil wish,
Without woman of evil eye,
Without malice, without envy, without *toirinn,*
Without hipped bear,
Without wilderness dog,
Without *scan foirinn,*★
Obtaining hold of the rich dainty
Into which this shall go.
Figwort of bright lights,
Fruitage to place therein,
With fruit, with grace, with joyance.

160   The figwort

I will pluck the figwort,
With the fullness of sea and land,
At the flow, not the ebb of the tide,
By thine hand, gentle Mary.

The kindly Colum directing me,
The holy Oran protecting me,
Whilst Bride of women beneficent
Shall put fruitage in the kine.

★A wild animal "of the border land."

As the King of kings ordained,
To put milk in breast and gland,
As the Being of life ordained,
To put sap in udder and teat.

In udder of badger,
In udder of reindeer,
In udder of sow,
In udder of mare.

In udder of sow,
In udder of heifer,
In udder of goat, ewe, and sheep,
Of roe, and of cow.

With milk, with cream, with substance,
With rutting, with begetting, with fruitfulness,
With female calves excelling,
With progeny, with joyance, with blessing.

Without man of evil wish,
Without woman of evil eye,
Without malice, without envy,
Without one evil.

In name of the apostles twelve,
In name of the Mother of God,
In name of Christ Himself,
And of Patrick.

161   The charm of the figwort

I will cull the figwort,
Of thousand blessings, of thousand virtues,
The calm Bride endowing it to me,
The fair Mary enriching it to me,
      The great Mary, aid-Mother of the people.

Came the nine joys,
With the nine waves,
To cull the figwort,
Of thousand blessings, of thousand virtues:
    Of thousand blessings, of thousand virtues.

The arm of Christ about me,
The face of Christ before me,
The shade of Christ over me,
My noble plant is being culled:
    My noble plant is being culled.

In name of the Father of wisdom,
In name of the Christ of Pasch,
In name of the Spirit of grace,
Who in the struggles of my death,
Will not leave me till Doom:
    Who in the struggles of my death,
    Will not leave me till Doom.

162   **The fairy wort**

Pluck will I the fairy wort,
With expectation from the fairy bower,
To overcome every oppression,
As long as it be fairy wort.

Fairy wort, fairy wort,
I envy the one who has thee,
There is nothing the sun encircles,
But is to her a sure victory.

Pluck will I mine honoured plant
Plucked by the great Mary, helpful Mother of the people,
To cast off me every tale of scandal and flippancy,
Ill-life, ill-love, ill-luck,
Hatred, falsity, fraud and vexation,
Till I go in the cold grave beneath the sod.

163   The yarrow

I will pluck the yarrow fair,
That more benign shall be my face,
That more warm shall be my lips,
That more chaste shall be my speech,
Be my speech the beams of the sun,
Be my lips the sap of the strawberry.

May I be an isle in the sea,
May I be a hill on the shore,
May I be a star in waning of the moon,
May I be a staff to the weak,
Wound can I every man,
Wound can no man me.

164   The yarrow

I will pluck the yarrow fair,
That more brave shall be my hand,
That more warm shall be my lips,
That more swift shall be my foot;
May I an island be at sea,
May I a rock be on land,
That I can afflict any man,
No man can afflict me.

165   Saint John's wort

I will cull my plantlet,
As a prayer to my King,
To quiet the wrath of men of blood,
To check the wiles of wanton women.

I will cull my plantlet,
As a prayer to my King,
That mine may be its power
Over all I see.

I will cull my plantlet,
As a prayer to the Three,
Beneath the shade of the Triune of grace,
And of Mary the Mother of Jesu.

166   St. Columba's plant

I will pluck what I meet,
As in communion with my saint,
To stop the wiles of wily men,
And the arts of foolish women.

I will pluck my Columba plant,
As a prayer to my King,
That mine be the power of Columba's plant,
Over every one I see.

I will pluck the leaf above,
As ordained of the High King,
In name of the Three of glory,
And of Mary, Mother of Christ.

167   St. Columba's plant

Plantlet of Columba,
Without seeking, without searching,
Plantlet of Columba,
Under my arm for ever!

For luck of men,
For luck of means,

For luck of wish,
For luck of sheep,
For luck of goats,
For luck of birds,
For luck of fields,
For luck of shellfish,
For luck of fish,
For luck of produce and kine,
For luck of progeny and people,
For luck of battle and victory,
On land, on sea, on ocean,
Through the Three on high,
Through the Three a-nigh,
Through the Three eternal,
Plantlet of Columba,
I cull thee now,
    I cull thee now.

168   Saint John's wort

Saint John's wort, Saint John's wort,
My envy whosoever has thee,
I will pluck thee with my right hand,
I will preserve thee with my left hand,
Whoso findeth thee in the cattle fold,
Shall never be without kine.

169   The aspen

Malison be on thee, O aspen tree!
On thee was crucified the King of the mountains,
In whom were driven the nails without clench,
And that driving crucifying was exceeding sore;
    That driving crucifying was exceeding sore.

Malison be on thee, O aspen hard!
On thee was crucified the King of glory,
Sacrifice of Truth, Lamb without blemish,
His blood in streams downpouring;
     His blood in streams downpouring.

Malison be on thee, O aspen cursed!
On thee was crucified the King of kings,
And malison be on the eye that seeth thee,
If it maledict thee not, thou aspen cursed;
     If it maledict thee not, thou aspen cursed!

170   Shamrock of luck

Thou shamrock of good omens,
Beneath the bank growing
Whereon stood the gracious Mary,
The Mother of God.

The seven joys are,
Without evil traces,
On thee, peerless one
Of the sunbeams:

     Joy of health,
     Joy of friends,
     Joy of kine,
     Joy of sheep,
     Joy of sons, and
     Daughters fair,
     Joy of peace,
     Joy of God!

The four leaves of the straight stem,
Of the straight stem from the root of the hundred rootlets,
Thou shamrock of promise on Mary's Day,
Bounty and blessing thou art at all times.

171 The shamrock of power

Thou shamrock of foliage,
Thou shamrock of power,
Thou shamrock of foliage,
Which Mary had under the bank,
Thou shamrock of my love,
Of most beauteous hue,
I would choose thee in death,
To grow on my grave,
I would choose thee in death,
To grow on my grave.

172 The *mòthan*

I will pluck the gracious *mòthan*,
As plucked the victorious King of the universe;
In name of Father and of Son and of Spirit everlasting,
    Bride, and Mary, and Michael, before me.

I in the field of red conflict,
In which every wrath and fury are quelled,
The cause of all joy and gladness,
    The shield of the Lord protecting me.

173 The *mòthan*

Pluck will I the *mòthan*,
Plant of the nine joints,
Pluck will I and vow me,
    To noble Bride and her Fosterling.

Pluck will I the *mòthan*,
As ordained of the King of power,

Pluck will I and vow me,
    To great Mary and her Son.

Pluck will I the *mòthan,*
As ordained of the King of life,
To overcome all oppression,
    And the spell of evil eye.

174   The *mòthan*

I will pluck the gracious *mòthan,*
Plant most precious in the field,
That mine be the holiness of the seven priests,
And the eloquence that is within them.

★   ★   ★

That mine be their wisdom and their counsel,
While the *mòthan* is mine.

175   The passion-flower of virtues

Thou passion-flower of virtues beloved,
Sanctified by the holy blood of the Lamb,
Son of Mary fair, Foster Son of Bride of kine,
Son of Mary great, helpful Mother of the people.

There is no earth, no land,
There is no lake, no ocean,
There is no pool, no water,
There is no forest, no steep,
That is not to me full safe,
By the protection of the passion-flower of virtues,
    But is to me full safe,
    By the protection of the passion-flower of virtues.

176   The club-moss

The club-moss is on my person,
No harm nor mishap can me befall;
No sprite shall slay me, no arrow shall wound me,
No fay nor dun water-nymph shall tear me.

177   The red-palmed

Christ walking with His apostles,
And breaking silence He said:
"What is the name of this plant?"
"The name of this plant is
The red-palmed,
The right palm of God the Son
        And His left foot."

178   The catkin wool

I will pluck the catkin wool,
As plucked the Mother of Christ through her palm,
For luck, for kine, for milking,
For herds, for increase, for cattle,
Without loss of lamb, without loss of sheep,
Without loss of goat, without loss of mare,
Without loss of cow, without loss of calf,
Without loss of means, without loss of friends,
        From the bosom of the God of life,
        And the courses together.

179   The catkin wool

Pluck will I myself the catkin wool,
The lint the lovely Bride culled through her palm,
For success, for cattle, for increase,
For pairing, for uddering, for milking,
For female calves, white bellied,
As was spoken in the prophecy.

180   Incantation of the red water

In name of the Father of love,
In name of the Son of sorrow,
In name of the Sacred Spirit.
    Amen.

Great wave, red wave,
Strength of sea, strength of ocean,
The nine wells of Mac-Lir,
Help on thee to pour,
Put stop to thy blood,
Put flood to thy urine.
    [*The name.*]

181   Red water charm

I am now on the plain,
Reducing wrath and fury,
Making the charm of the red water,
To the beauteous black cow.

For milk, for milk substance, for milk produce,
For whisked whey, for milk riches,
For curdled milk, for milk plenty,
For butter, for cheese, for curds.

For progeny and prosperity,
For rutting time and rutting,
For desire and kine,
For passion and prosperity.

The nine wells of Mac-Lir,
Relief on thee to pour,
Put stop to thy blood,
Put run to thy urine,
Thou cow of cows, black cow.

>   Great sea,
>   Red cascade
>   Stop blood,
>   Flow urine.

182   The gravel charm

I have a charm for the gravel disease,
    For the disease that is perverse;
I have a charm for the red disease,
    For the disease that is irritating.

As runs a river cold,
    As grinds a rapid mill,
Thou who didst ordain land and sea,
    Cease the blood and let flow the urine.

In name of Father, and of Son,
    In name of Holy Spirit.

183   The strangles

"A horse in strangles,"
Quoth Columba.

"I will turn it,"
Said Christ.

"On Sunday morning?"
Quoth Columba.

"Ere rise of sun,"
Said Christ.

"Three pillars in the well,"
Quoth Columba.

"I will lift them,"
Said Christ.

"Will that heal him?"
Quoth John the Baptist.

"Assuredly,"
Said Christ.

184   The spell of the fox

Be the spell of the wood-dog,
On the feet of the fox,
On his heart, on his liver,
On his gullet of greediness,
On his surpassing pointed teeth,
On the bend of his stomach.

Be the charm of the Lord upon the sheep-kind,
The charm of Christ kindly-white, mild-white,
The charm of Mary lovely-fair, tender-fair,
Against dogs, against birds, against mankind,

Against fairy dogs, against world dogs,
Of the world hither, of the world thither.

185   Prayer of the cattlefold

I drive the kine within
The gateway of the herds,
On voice of the dead,
On voice of bull,
On voice of pairing,
On voice of grayling cow
White-headed, strong-headed, of udder.
Be the big stone of the base of the couple
Without ceasing, without decreasing,
As a full-weighted tether
Trailing from the hunch of your rump,
Till bright daylight comes in tomorrow.

The Father, the Son, the Holy Spirit,
Save you, and shield you, and tend you,
Till I or mine shall meet you again.

186   The ditch of Mary

Ditch of Mary,
Ditch of Mary;
Heron legs,
Heron legs;
Ditch of Mary,
Ditch of Mary;
Heron legs under you,
Bridge of warranty before you.

Mary placed a wand in it,
Bride placed a hand in it,

Columba placed a foot in it,
Patrick placed a cold stone.

> Ditch of Mary,
> Ditch of Mary;
> Heron legs,
> Heron legs;
> Ditch of Mary,
> Ditch of Mary;

Heron legs under you,
Bridge of warranty before you.

Muirel placed myrrh in it,
Uriel placed honey in it,
Muirinn placed wine in it,
And Michael placed in it power.

> Ditch of Mary,
> Ditch of Mary;
> Heron legs,
> Heron legs;
> Ditch of Mary,
> Ditch of Mary;

Heron legs under you,
Bridge of warranty before you.

187   The hind

Peter and Paul were passing by,
While a hind in the path was bearing a fawn;
"A hind is bearing there," said Peter;
"I see it is so," said Paul.

"As her foliage falls from the tree,
So may her placenta fall to the ground,
In name of the Father of love and of the Son of grace,
And of the Spirit of loving wisdom;

Father of love and Son of grace,
And Spirit of loving wisdom."

188   Columba, Peter, and Paul

A day as I was going to Rome,
I forgathered with Columba, Peter, and Paul,
The talk that they had and that happened in their
      mouths,
Was loud-lunged, white-bellied, female calves,
As was spoken in the prophecy,
On this foundation for a year and a day,
Through the bosom of the God of life and all the hosts,
Chief of chiefs and of the everlasting Powers above.

189   The indigestion spell

The spell made of Columba,
To the one cow of the woman,
For the *crailleach,* for the gum disease,
For the bag, for the *colg,*
For the indigestion;

For the flux disease,
For the cud disease,
For the *mir* disease,
For the *tolg* disease,
For the surfeit;

For the *cil* disease,
For the *mil* disease,
For the water disease,
For the red disease,
For the madness;

I will cleave the *crailleach,*
I will cleave the gum disease,
I will cleave the bag,
I will cleave the *colg,*
And I will kill the indigestion;

I will cleave the flux,
I will cleave the cud,
I will cleave the *mir,*
I will cleave the *tolg,*
And drive away the surfeit;

I will cleave the *cil,*
I will cleave the *mil,*
I will cleave the water,
I will cleave the red,
And wither will the madness.

190   Cud chewing charm

If thou hast eaten the grass of the nine bens,
Of the nine fells, of the nine hillocks,
If thou hast drunk the water of the nine falls,
Of the nine streams, of the nine lakelets,
Poor "Gruaigein" of the hard paunch,
Loved one, chew thou thy cud.
Poor "Gruaigein" of the hard paunch,
Loved one, chew thou thy cud.

191   Charm of the churn

Come will the free, come;
Come will the bond, come;
Come will the bells, come;
Come will the maers, come;

Come will the blade, come;
Come will the sharp, come;
Come will the hounds, come;
Come will the wild, come;
Come will the mild, come;
Come will the kind, come;
Come will the loving, come;
Come will the squint, come;
Come will he of the yellow cap,
That will set the churn a-running.

The free will come,
The bond will come,
The bells will come,
The maers will come,
The blades will come,
The sharp will come,
The hounds will come,
The wild will come,
The mild will come,
The kind will come,
The loving will come,
The devious will come,
The brim-full of the globe will come,
To set the churn a-running;
The kindly Columba will come in his array,
And the golden-haired Bride of the kine.

A splash is here,
A plash is here,
A plash is here,
A splash is here,
A crash is here,
A squash is here,
A squash is here,
A crash is here,
A big soft snail is here,
The sap of each of the cows is here,

A thing better than honey and spruce,
A bogle yellow and fresh is here.

A thing better than right is here,
The fist of the big priest is here,
A thing better than the carcase is here,
The head of the dead man is here,
A thing better than wine is here,
The full of the cog of Caristine
Of live things soft and fair are here,
        Of live things soft and fair are here.

Come, thou churn, come;
Come, thou churn, come;
Come, thou life; come, thou breath;
Come, thou churn, come;
Come, thou churn, come;
Come, thou cuckoo; come, thou jackdaw;
Come, thou churn, come;
Come, thou churn, come;
Come will the little lark from the sky,
Come will the little carlin of the black-cap.
Come, thou churn, come;
Come, thou churn, come;
Come will the merle, come will the mavis;
Come will the music from the bower;
Come, thou churn, come;
Come, thou churn, come;
Come, thou wild cat,
To ease thy throat;
Come, thou churn, come;
Come, thou churn, come.

Come, thou hound, and quench thy thirst;
Come, thou churn, come;
Come, thou churn, come;

Come, thou poor; come, thou naked;
Come, thou churn, come;
Come, thou churn, come;
Come, ye alms-deserver
Of most distressful moan;
Come, thou churn, come;
Come, thou churn, come;
Come, each hungry creature,
And satisfy the thirst of thy body.

Come, thou churn, come;
Come, thou churn, come;
It is the God of the elements who bestowed on us,
And not the charm of a carlin with plant.
Come, thou churn, come;
Come, thou churn, come;
Come, thou fair-white Mary,
And endow to me my means;
Come, thou churn, come;
Come, thou churn, come;
Come, thou beauteous Bride,
And bless the substance of my kine.

Come, thou churn, come;
Come, thou churn, come;
The churning made of Mary,
In the fastness of the glen,
To decrease her milk,
To increase her butter;
Buttermilk to wrist,
Butter to elbow;
  Come, thou churn, come;
  Come, thou churn, come.

192   The charm sent of Mary

The charm sent of Mary Virgin
To the nun who was dwelling
On the floor of the glen,
On the cold high moors:
    On the floor of the glen,
    On the cold high moors.

She put spell to saliva,
To increase her butter,
To decrease her milk,
To make plentiful her food:
    To increase her butter,
    To decrease her milk,
    To make plentiful her food.

193   The wicked who would me harm

The wicked who would do me harm
May he take the throat disease,
Globularly, spirally, circularly,
Fluxy, pellety, horny-grim.

Be it harder than the stone,
Be it blacker than the coal,
Be it swifter than the duck,
Be it heavier than the lead.

Be it fiercer, fiercer, sharper, harsher, more malignant,
Than the hard, wound-quivering holly,
Be it sourer than the sained, lustrous, bitter, salt salt,
Seven seven times.

Oscillating thither,
Undulating hither,
Staggering downwards,
Floundering upwards.

Drivelling outwards,
Snivelling inwards,
Oft hurrying out,
Seldom coming in.

A wisp the portion of each hand,
A foot in the base of each pillar,
A leg the prop of each jamb,
A flux driving and dragging him.

A dysentery of blood from heart, from form, from bones,
From the liver, from the lobe, from the lungs,
And a searching of veins, of throat, and of kidneys,
To my contemners and traducers.

In name of the God of might,
Who warded from me every evil,
And who shielded me in strength
From the net of my breakers
    And destroyers.

194 Augury of Mary

God over me, God under me,
God before me, God behind me,
I on Thy path, O God,
    Thou, O God, in my steps.

The augury made of Mary to her Son,
The offering made of Bride through her palm,
Sawest Thou it, King of life?
    Said the King of life that He saw.

The augury made by Mary for her own offspring,
When He was for a space amissing,
Knowledge of truth, not knowledge of falsehood,
    That I shall truly see all my quest.

Son of beauteous Mary, King of life,
Give Thou me eyes to see all my quest,
With grace that shall never fail, before me,
That shall never quench nor dim.

A CATALOG OF SELECTED DOVER
BOOKS IN ALL FIELDS OF INTEREST

CONCERNING THE SPIRITUAL IN ART, Wassily Kandinsky. Pioneering work by father of abstract art. Thoughts on color theory, nature of art. Analysis of earlier masters. 12 illustrations. 80pp. of text. 5⅜ x 8½.   0-486-23411-8

CELTIC ART: The Methods of Construction, George Bain. Simple geometric techniques for making Celtic interlacements, spirals, Kells-type initials, animals, humans, etc. Over 500 illustrations. 160pp. 9 x 12. (Available in U.S. only.)   0-486-22923-8

AN ATLAS OF ANATOMY FOR ARTISTS, Fritz Schider. Most thorough reference work on art anatomy in the world. Hundreds of illustrations, including selections from works by Vesalius, Leonardo, Goya, Ingres, Michelangelo, others. 593 illustrations. 192pp. 7⅛ x 10¼.   0-486-20241-0

CELTIC HAND STROKE-BY-STROKE (Irish Half-Uncial from "The Book of Kells"): An Arthur Baker Calligraphy Manual, Arthur Baker. Complete guide to creating each letter of the alphabet in distinctive Celtic manner. Covers hand position, strokes, pens, inks, paper, more. Illustrated. 48pp. 8¼ x 11.   0-486-24336-2

EASY ORIGAMI, John Montroll. Charming collection of 32 projects (hat, cup, pelican, piano, swan, many more) specially designed for the novice origami hobbyist. Clearly illustrated easy-to-follow instructions insure that even beginning papercrafters will achieve successful results. 48pp. 8¼ x 11.   0-486-27298-2

BLOOMINGDALE'S ILLUSTRATED 1886 CATALOG: Fashions, Dry Goods and Housewares, Bloomingdale Brothers. Famed merchants' extremely rare catalog depicting about 1,700 products: clothing, housewares, firearms, dry goods, jewelry, more. Invaluable for dating, identifying vintage items. Also, copyright-free graphics for artists, designers. Co-published with Henry Ford Museum & Greenfield Village. 160pp. 8¼ x 11.   0-486-25780-0

THE ART OF WORLDLY WISDOM, Baltasar Gracian. "Think with the few and speak with the many," "Friends are a second existence," and "Be able to forget" are among this 1637 volume's 300 pithy maxims. A perfect source of mental and spiritual refreshment, it can be opened at random and appreciated either in brief or at length. 128pp. 5⅜ x 8½.   0-486-44034-6

JOHNSON'S DICTIONARY: A Modern Selection, Samuel Johnson (E. L. McAdam and George Milne, eds.). This modern version reduces the original 1755 edition's 2,300 pages of definitions and literary examples to a more manageable length, retaining the verbal pleasure and historical curiosity of the original. 480pp. 5³⁄₁₆ x 8¼.   0-486-44089-3

ADVENTURES OF HUCKLEBERRY FINN, Mark Twain, Illustrated by E. W. Kemble. A work of eternal richness and complexity, a source of ongoing critical debate, and a literary landmark, Twain's 1885 masterpiece about a barefoot boy's journey of self-discovery has enthralled readers around the world. This handsome clothbound reproduction of the first edition features all 174 of the original black-and-white illustrations. 368pp. 5⅜ x 8½.   0-486-44322-1

STICKLEY CRAFTSMAN FURNITURE CATALOGS, Gustav Stickley and L. & J. G. Stickley. Beautiful, functional furniture in two authentic catalogs from 1910. 594 illustrations, including 277 photos, show settles, rockers, armchairs, reclining chairs, bookcases, desks, tables. 183pp. 6½ x 9¼. 0-486-23838-5

AMERICAN LOCOMOTIVES IN HISTORIC PHOTOGRAPHS: 1858 to 1949, Ron Ziel (ed.). A rare collection of 126 meticulously detailed official photographs, called "builder portraits," of American locomotives that majestically chronicle the rise of steam locomotive power in America. Introduction. Detailed captions. xi+ 129pp. 9 x 12. 0-486-27393-8

AMERICA'S LIGHTHOUSES: An Illustrated History, Francis Ross Holland, Jr. Delightfully written, profusely illustrated fact-filled survey of over 200 American light-houses since 1716. History, anecdotes, technological advances, more. 240pp. 8 x 10¾. 0-486-25576-X

TOWARDS A NEW ARCHITECTURE, Le Corbusier. Pioneering manifesto by founder of "International School." Technical and aesthetic theories, views of industry, economics, relation of form to function, "mass-production split" and much more. Profusely illustrated. 320pp. 6⅛ x 9¼. (Available in U.S. only.) 0-486-25023-7

HOW THE OTHER HALF LIVES, Jacob Riis. Famous journalistic record, exposing poverty and degradation of New York slums around 1900, by major social reformer. 100 striking and influential photographs. 233pp. 10 x 7⅞. 0-486-22012-5

FRUIT KEY AND TWIG KEY TO TREES AND SHRUBS, William M. Harlow. One of the handiest and most widely used identification aids. Fruit key covers 120 deciduous and evergreen species; twig key 160 deciduous species. Easily used. Over 300 photographs. 126pp. 5⅜ x 8½. 0-486-20511-8

COMMON BIRD SONGS, Dr. Donald J. Borror. Songs of 60 most common U.S. birds: robins, sparrows, cardinals, bluejays, finches, more—arranged in order of increasing complexity. Up to 9 variations of songs of each species.
Cassette and manual 0-486-99911-4

ORCHIDS AS HOUSE PLANTS, Rebecca Tyson Northen. Grow cattleyas and many other kinds of orchids—in a window, in a case, or under artificial light. 63 illustrations. 148pp. 5⅜ x 8½. 0-486-23261-1

MONSTER MAZES, Dave Phillips. Masterful mazes at four levels of difficulty. Avoid deadly perils and evil creatures to find magical treasures. Solutions for all 32 exciting illustrated puzzles. 48pp. 8¼ x 11. 0-486-26005-4

MOZART'S DON GIOVANNI (DOVER OPERA LIBRETTO SERIES), Wolfgang Amadeus Mozart. Introduced and translated by Ellen H. Bleiler. Standard Italian libretto, with complete English translation. Convenient and thoroughly portable—an ideal companion for reading along with a recording or the performance itself. Introduction. List of characters. Plot summary. 121pp. 5¼ x 8½. 0-486-24944-1

FRANK LLOYD WRIGHT'S DANA HOUSE, Donald Hoffmann. Pictorial essay of residential masterpiece with over 160 interior and exterior photos, plans, elevations, sketches and studies. 128pp. 9¼ x 10¾. 0-486-29120-0

THE CLARINET AND CLARINET PLAYING, David Pino. Lively, comprehensive work features suggestions about technique, musicianship, and musical interpretation, as well as guidelines for teaching, making your own reeds, and preparing for public performance. Includes an intriguing look at clarinet history. "A godsend," *The Clarinet,* Journal of the International Clarinet Society. Appendixes. 7 illus. 320pp. 5⅜ x 8½. 0-486-40270-3

HOLLYWOOD GLAMOR PORTRAITS, John Kobal (ed.). 145 photos from 1926-49. Harlow, Gable, Bogart, Bacall; 94 stars in all. Full background on photographers, technical aspects. 160pp. 8⅜ x 11¼. 0-486-23352-9

THE RAVEN AND OTHER FAVORITE POEMS, Edgar Allan Poe. Over 40 of the author's most memorable poems: "The Bells," "Ulalume," "Israfel," "To Helen," "The Conqueror Worm," "Eldorado," "Annabel Lee," many more. Alphabetic lists of titles and first lines. 64pp. 5 3/16 x 8¼. 0-486-26685-0

PERSONAL MEMOIRS OF U. S. GRANT, Ulysses Simpson Grant. Intelligent, deeply moving firsthand account of Civil War campaigns, considered by many the finest military memoirs ever written. Includes letters, historic photographs, maps and more. 528pp. 6⅛ x 9¼. 0-486-28587-1

ANCIENT EGYPTIAN MATERIALS AND INDUSTRIES, A. Lucas and J. Harris. Fascinating, comprehensive, thoroughly documented text describes this ancient civilization's vast resources and the processes that incorporated them in daily life, including the use of animal products, building materials, cosmetics, perfumes and incense, fibers, glazed ware, glass and its manufacture, materials used in the mummification process, and much more. 544pp. 6 1/8 x 9 1/4. (Available in U.S. only.) 0-486-40446-3

RUSSIAN STORIES/RUSSKIE RASSKAZY: A Dual-Language Book, edited by Gleb Struve. Twelve tales by such masters as Chekhov, Tolstoy, Dostoevsky, Pushkin, others. Excellent word-for-word English translations on facing pages, plus teaching and study aids, Russian/English vocabulary, biographical/critical introductions, more. 416pp. 5⅜ x 8½. 0-486-26244-8

PHILADELPHIA THEN AND NOW: 60 Sites Photographed in the Past and Present, Kenneth Finkel and Susan Oyama. Rare photographs of City Hall, Logan Square, Independence Hall, Betsy Ross House, other landmarks juxtaposed with contemporary views. Captures changing face of historic city. Introduction. Captions. 128pp. 8¼ x 11. 0-486-25790-8

NORTH AMERICAN INDIAN LIFE: Customs and Traditions of 23 Tribes, Elsie Clews Parsons (ed.). 27 fictionalized essays by noted anthropologists examine religion, customs, government, additional facets of life among the Winnebago, Crow, Zuni, Eskimo, other tribes. 480pp. 6⅛ x 9¼. 0-486-27377-6

TECHNICAL MANUAL AND DICTIONARY OF CLASSICAL BALLET, Gail Grant. Defines, explains, comments on steps, movements, poses and concepts. 15-page pictorial section. Basic book for student, viewer. 127pp. 5⅜ x 8½. 0-486-21843-0

THE MALE AND FEMALE FIGURE IN MOTION: 60 Classic Photographic Sequences, Eadweard Muybridge. 60 true-action photographs of men and women walking, running, climbing, bending, turning, etc., reproduced from rare 19th-century masterpiece. vi + 121pp. 9 x 12. 0-486-24745-7

CATALOG OF DOVER BOOKS

LIGHT AND SHADE: A Classic Approach to Three-Dimensional Drawing, Mrs. Mary P. Merrifield. Handy reference clearly demonstrates principles of light and shade by revealing effects of common daylight, sunshine, and candle or artificial light on geometrical solids. 13 plates. 64pp. 5⅜ x 8½. 0-486-44143-1

ASTROLOGY AND ASTRONOMY: A Pictorial Archive of Signs and Symbols, Ernst and Johanna Lehner. Treasure trove of stories, lore, and myth, accompanied by more than 300 rare illustrations of planets, the Milky Way, signs of the zodiac, comets, meteors, and other astronomical phenomena. 192pp. 8⅜ x 11. 0-486-43981-X

JEWELRY MAKING: Techniques for Metal, Tim McCreight. Easy-to-follow instructions and carefully executed illustrations describe tools and techniques, use of gems and enamels, wire inlay, casting, and other topics. 72 line illustrations and diagrams. 176pp. 8¼ x 10⅞. 0-486-44043-5

MAKING BIRDHOUSES: Easy and Advanced Projects, Gladstone Califf. Easy-to-follow instructions include diagrams for everything from a one-room house for bluebirds to a forty-two-room structure for purple martins. 56 plates; 4 figures. 80pp. 8¾ x 6⅜. 0-486-44183-0

LITTLE BOOK OF LOG CABINS: How to Build and Furnish Them, William S. Wicks. Handy how-to manual, with instructions and illustrations for building cabins in the Adirondack style, fireplaces, stairways, furniture, beamed ceilings, and more. 102 line drawings. 96pp. 8¾ x 6⅜. 0-486-44259-4

THE SEASONS OF AMERICA PAST, Eric Sloane. From "sugaring time" and strawberry picking to Indian summer and fall harvest, a whole year's activities described in charming prose and enhanced with 79 of the author's own illustrations. 160pp. 8¼ x 11. 0-486-44220-9

THE METROPOLIS OF TOMORROW, Hugh Ferriss. Generous, prophetic vision of the metropolis of the future, as perceived in 1929. Powerful illustrations of towering structures, wide avenues, and rooftop parks–all features in many of today's modern cities. 59 illustrations. 144pp. 8¼ x 11. 0-486-43727-2

THE PATH TO ROME, Hilaire Belloc. This 1902 memoir abounds in lively vignettes from a vanished time, recounting a pilgrimage on foot across the Alps and Apennines in order to "see all Europe which the Christian Faith has saved." 77 of the author's original line drawings complement his sparkling prose. 272pp. 5⅜ x 8½. 0-486-44001-X

THE HISTORY OF RASSELAS: Prince of Abissinia, Samuel Johnson. Distinguished English writer attacks eighteenth-century optimism and man's unrealistic estimates of what life has to offer. 112pp. 5⅜ x 8½. 0-486-44094-X

A VOYAGE TO ARCTURUS, David Lindsay. A brilliant flight of pure fancy, where wild creatures crowd the fantastic landscape and demented torturers dominate victims with their bizarre mental powers. 272pp. 5⅜ x 8½. 0-486-44198-9

Paperbound unless otherwise indicated. Available at your book dealer, online at **www.doverpublications.com**, or by writing to Dept. GI, Dover Publications, Inc., 31 East 2nd Street, Mineola, NY 11501. For current price information or for free catalogs (please indicate field of interest), write to Dover Publications or log on to **www.doverpublications.com** and see every Dover book in print. Dover publishes more than 500 books each year on science, elementary and advanced mathematics, biology, music, art, literary history, social sciences, and other areas.